I0098846

Countryfied Chickens

A cautionary tale for anyone considering a move to the country

by CHAS ELLIOTT

8 GRANDKIDS

PUBLISHED BY

Eight Grandkids Publishing, L.L.C.

PO Box 2338

Chelan WA 98816

"Family" cover illustration and all other illustrations
by Marty Jaso.

Cover and book design by Jill St Michael.

Copyright © 2013,

by Eight Grandkids Publishing, L.L.C.

All rights reserved.

July 2013

First edition

ISBN-10: 0615827411

ISBN-13: 978-0615827414

This book is dedicated to the millions of small-town residents out there who willingly sacrifice such creature-comforts as hot, delivered pizza, to carry on the American tradition of getting as far away from other people as they possibly can.

CONTENTS

ACKNOWLEDGMENTS

There are usually some behind-the-scenes people who bring out the best in an author and help make sure that the book is as good as it can be. First and foremost, I must acknowledge my wife, Sandi, who actually lived the book and helped me see there was a fun story to be told – even though some events did not seem so fun at the time. My sister-in-law, Barb, deserves a big thank you not only for the boxes she helped us pack up but also for the moral support she provided throughout the ordeal. She also generously helped us to make our new house inhabitable. Our contractor, Paul, got a lot more work than he bargained for and he deserves a big thank you for hanging in there until the job was done, and for his good humor. We poked a little fun at my son-in-law John, who drove the Mother of All Moving Trucks, but we are grateful for the time he spent helping us move, not to mention the improvements he has made around the house since we moved in. Also special thanks to his wife and our daughter Tara, as well as her kids, for all the help they gave us during the move-in. As the book went into production, two people helped us immensely: Marty Jaso, who did all of the ingenious drawings you see in this book as well as the cover illustration, and Jill St Michael, who designed the book's layout, including what we think is a very snappy cover.

I also would be remiss if I didn't thank Oscar (not is real name), the newly minted real estate agent who was just trying to do a good job and probably didn't realize I was taking copious notes every step of the way. We poked a little fun at his learning curve, but ultimately he got the job done and we're sure he will have a great career in real estate. Thanks also to the CHIPS officer who detained our son-in-law, the inspectors who, shall we say, missed a few things, and of course a big shout-out to the lending company that made us sweat bullets while ultimately helping us disclose to the general public what is known as the "48 Hour Rule". Without these and other contributors, this book wouldn't have been nearly so much fun to write.

1

It's the American Way

It's a time-honored tradition in the United States of America to want to move to the country. The pilgrims landed and somebody said "Let's move a little further from the sea where it's not quite so crowded." Then as they moved further from the sea it became evident that urban sprawl had already begun as Indians – excuse us, Native Americans – were found to have grabbed up a lot of the prime real estate with little regard for local zoning laws, setting up any number of teepees that quite obviously were built against code.

Then someone said, "Let's move further away from the Native Americans."

So then began centuries of migration across North America where folks would move out west to places like St. Louis, and then realize they hadn't moved quite far enough to be in the real boonies. So then came the wagon trains that transported settlers even further west where, along the way, they'd come across a few random forts with U.S. Calvary and figure, okay, we can settle someplace around this fort but we really don't want to be near all the noise and congestion of the fort so we'll move a little further out in the country.

And then a few of the settlers would be scalped and figure the boonies weren't all they were cracked up to be, and they'd move back closer to the forts. But over time, the cities and towns that grew up alongside the forts became more crowded and residents became impatient as they would have to stand two or three deep in line at the General Store. Parking was almost non-existent as every itinerant cowboy you could imagine would park his horse just anywhere, sometimes leaving it all night while visiting the ladies upstairs in the local saloon. You could never find a Sheriff when you needed one because population had outgrown the local infrastructure. Pesky neighbors would shoot first and ask questions later.

Soon it was obvious that the only solution was to migrate even further into the country. People built little houses on big swaths of land they got for almost free from the federal government, the country's first real Economic Stimulus plan. These lands became ranches, and these ranches became estates, and these estates became suburban villages with a Starbucks on every third block. For some, that meant it was time to migrate even further.

Which brings us to modern-day America where the quest to outrun Starbucks means that you have to get serious about your migration plans because, in some parts of this country, we're running out of boonies.

We speak from experience. We have just gone through the ultimate migration from suburban San Diego to a seemingly remote wilderness area in North Central Washington state and are living proof that it's possible to move to the country and still have access to modern-day conveniences and civilization. We have running water, indoor toilets and DISH TV – what else could you ever ask for?

Maybe you, too, have thought about how nice it would be to leave behind the traffic jams and frenetic pace of the Big City for the tranquility of the country. Maybe you're tired of two-hour daily commutes to work. Maybe you're tired of neighbors living so close they could reach over to your property and hold hands with you as you say blessings. Maybe you always wanted to add a garage but the largest structure you can accommodate is a bird-feeder. Maybe you would just like to lay naked in your backyard without having to register as a sex offender.

These are all good reasons to move to the country. But are you REALLY ready for a move to the country? Here's how you tell:

- If your weekly trip to Costco is more important to you than your weekly trip to church, you may not be ready for a move to the country.

- If you order your coffee size in Italian, you may not be ready for a move to the country.

- If you do your nails more than seasonally, you may not be ready for a move to the country.

- If you insist on wearing a different change of clothes each day, you may not be ready for a move to the country.

- If you find animal poop disgusting, you may not be ready for a move to the country.

- If you like to order pizza for delivery, you may not be ready for a move to the country.

- If you don't know where your water comes from, or where your sewage goes, you may not be ready for a move to the country.

- If you don't believe yard work is a calling, you may not be ready for a move to the country.

- If sporadic gunfire makes you nervous, you may not be ready for a move to the country.

- If you don't consider dial-up your preferred internet technology, you may not be ready for a move to the country.

- If Walmart is not your favorite designer clothing label, you may not be ready for a move to the country.

- If you would choose a BMW 7 series over a four-wheeler with a snowplow, you may not be ready for a move to the country.

- If ballet is higher on your bucket list than monster trucks, you may not be ready for a move to the country.

If you've passed these initial tests, congratulations – you now qualify for a move to the country and we'll do everything we can to talk you out of it (just kidding). We look back now at how innocent we were just months ago as we contemplated this great move and think of all the lessons we have learned since then. You might think we were pre-destined to live in the country but, to tell you the truth, we got here through lots of fits and starts and, as card-carrying city people, there were many times we almost chickened out.

But we made it – we're now living in the country. We're living proof that you should always "be careful what you wish for".

2

Sunshine vs. Kids

We've lived our adult lives in suburbia, most recently near San Diego, California, where we had settled into a nice four-bedroom house with the requisite California swimming pool and a view of the valley that surrounds the city of San Marcos. This was actually a place that San Diego people once moved to in order to get out in the country, but population growth quickly converted the local farmlands into new subdivisions which quickly begat new businesses which quickly took the city past the two most important milestones of urban development in 21st Century America: a Starbucks and a Costco. Today, San Marcos has three Starbucks stores, one giant recently remodeled Costco and three token farmers to remind people what life in San Marcos used to be like.

Now before you get the wrong idea, none of this was particularly objectionable to us – yes, you had to pack an overnight bag for a trip to the DMV and, yes, parents had to be bussed into school events because there was no parking within a seven-mile radius and, yes, most dinner reservations had to be made at least six months in advance, but these are things you learn to accept when living in suburbia. You learn to accept the fact that your house will be pretty much like your neighbor's house and that the architects of these subdivisions stayed up nights figuring out how to position the houses so that each and every house has an unobstructed view into the neighbor's bathroom.

This is what you give up when you want to make a quick run to a big-box store or a fast-food joint, or want to have a colonoscopy without turning it into a weekend getaway. Everything's close by when you live in suburbia and it's just unfortunate that the number one requirement for having all those things handy and easily accessible is more people. For many, the ideal American city would be a whole bunch of stores and restaurants, about 45 fire stations and maybe 250 people, all carefully vetted through rigorous FBI background checks.

As I mentioned, we didn't particularly dislike our suburban life and, after 14 years in the San Diego area, had set down roots just about as deep as most people in that city. San Diego people, by the way, all come from other places – we had a neighbor who grew up in San Diego, but apparently he was the only one and must have been dropped there by a container ship or something because we never met anyone else who could document a childhood in San Diego. Nevertheless, you do get attached to a place and the rumors about San Diego's warm and sunny weather are true. We were in no rush to leave.

But then life got in the way and we suddenly remembered we had aging parents, a daughter and son-in-law and a brood of eight grandchildren all still back in our home state of Washington. This was a big problem. Aged parents and families of 10 don't travel that well or often, so the traveling was mostly done from our end. Air fare became the second biggest household budget item, right behind our mortgage. Birthdays were missed, school events unattended and grandkids' names were forgotten. We got to thinking that, hey, if we didn't start seeing these people more often they'd forget OUR names. We'd show up to have them take us to the rest home and the response would be: "Now who exactly are you?"

The move from California to Washington took years to germinate because, as we all know, guilt doesn't come all at once and has to be carefully cultivated until it grows into something that causes you to inexplicably abandon the reasonable (warm, sunny Southern California, swimming pool, etc.) for the radical (cold winters). We would flirt with the idea, looking at real estate sites on the internet, mentally computing whether we could afford an even nicer house in Washington than we had in California. There was a time when California real estate was worth a lot more, you know. Unfortunately, that was sometime during the Cold War.

For the longest time we were fixated on waterfront. Why, I'm not exactly sure. The idea sounds great and we could envision ourselves on an island in Puget Sound someplace where we would spend our Golden years watching the boats and the seabirds. We'd have the grandkids come over and dig a few buckets of sand and lay in our hammocks and watch. We'd even get a boat and have it tied up to our own dock and then, every three years or so when the sun appears over Puget Sound, we would cruise into the sunset.

But then we started to do a little figuring. First, we have had some experience living in the Seattle area and whenever we play word association games, the word that always seems to go with Seattle is "gray." Okay, many of my Seattle friends would point out that "the bluest skies you'll ever see" are in Seattle – and that's probably true. It's just that they are pretty much a once-in-a-lifetime experience. Even the most luxurious beachfront estates somehow don't look the same with dark clouds, lightning bolts and real-live cats and dogs falling from the clouds.

Then we started computing our mortgage payments on those dark, foreboding waterfront properties and realized that the payments would be something akin to buying one small car per month and that, in reality, by the time we were headed for the rest home, our principal on this property might have been reduced by approximately five dollars and 95 cents, leaving the rest for our daughter and her husband to pay off while sending eight kids to college. "Gee thanks Mom and Dad, the kids WERE headed for Harvard but now we have to send them to the School for Day Laborers because we have to pay off this damn, dark, foreboding waterfront house."

So we decided to regroup. The grandkids were in Seattle, all right, and living elsewhere in Washington would cut down on our visits with the kids. But was it really that important that we see them collect every Award for Perfect Attendance? Were we shirking our responsibilities by blowing off our grandkids' extra-curricular activities? Wouldn't we still earn the Good Grandparents Seal of Approval if we showed up for birthdays and special events but did not set up a 24-hour on-call babysitting service for our beloved daughter and son-in-law?

The reason we asked ourselves all these questions is that we had it on good authority that the sun actually comes out in Central Washington, where our aging parents were located. We knew that for a fact because we had grown up in the Wenatchee area, a mid-size town that in many ways has not changed much since we left in the early 70's. There are more fast-food joints, big-box stores and traffic than the 70's, but the small-town values seem to remain pretty much intact. It's not quite Andy and Barney, but the only thing really missing is the southern accent.

So what a concept – move to Washington and not have to put up with the rain. Okay, winters can be cold in Central Washington but that's what ski parkas and long underwear are for. We'll get to fire up the 4-wheel drive for the first time since we bought our Jeep. We'll go sledding. We'll go skiing. We'll go to the hospital when we break our brittle bones. This will be fun!

3

Your Real Estate Agent

Okay, let's reset the scene: My wife and I and our 12-year-old daughter have been living with guilt the past several years as we bask in San Diego sunshine while our aging parents, our other daughter and her husband, and our eight grandkids somehow get by without us in Washington state. Visa cards are maxed out with air fare and we're still sharing most family events by phone or Skype. We have long considered moving close to our grandkids in rainy Seattle but some semblance of reason has finally taken hold and we are considering a move to Central Washington instead. Our cover story is we're moving there to take care of aging parents, but we've also factored in the desire to see a modicum of sunshine in our Golden years.

There is one other motivating factor for this impending move: trees. As much as we love San Diego, its sunshine and beaches, the region just seems devoid of trees. Not palm trees or eucalyptus – of which there are many – but good old-fashioned evergreens, the tall and stately kind that feel like an honest-to-goodness forest. Every time we'd visit Washington from Southern California we'd gravitate to the mountains and the forests where we would breathe in the scented air and listen to the lazy, bubbling streams or marvel at the cascading torrents of water raging down the Cascade Mountain rivers and surmise that if only San Diego had these natural resources, it would be heaven on earth.

And if only San Diego had these natural resources it, too, would be rainy.

So, grandkids, aging parents, trees – they were all pretty powerful motivators that, over time, insidiously took over our mental faculties to the degree that we were getting serious about leaving friends and our glorious sun-drenched life in San Diego to move to the wilds of North Central Washington. At this point we got a little more serious about looking at homes that were for sale in Wenatchee.

The thing about shopping for real estate is that everyone starts out asking about twice what their house is really worth. But when people want to buy YOUR house, it's not worth the land it was built on. These two laws of real estate are reconciled by what is known as the Real Estate Agent. First there's the seller's agent, whose job is to sit the home-seller down and break the news to him that he does not own the Taj Mahal: "Yes, Mr. Jones, the hand-carved statue of Arnold Schwarzenegger certainly adds to the beauty of your foyer and there is no question that the miniature Sleeping Beauty Castle with water-filled moat represents a great value for the buyers, but the reality is no one in their right mind will actually pay money for this dump. Only I, in my infinite wisdom and vast experience, will ever find you a buyer."

On the other side of the transaction is the buyer's agent, whose job is to show you at least 129 different properties and hope that the law of averages will kick in and he'll convince you to buy one of them. There is a delicate dance that takes place during this part of your home search because the buyer's agent has to at least appear that he's listening to what you want. Say you want a four-bedroom with a swimming pool and he takes you to a two-bedroom with a horse barn. "As you see, Mr. Jones, this house doesn't have four FOR-MAL bedrooms, but I think this china closet could easily convert to one additional bedroom and look at how big that living room is! You could easily add a futon sleeper there, and just out the window you can see your very own horse trough, the perfect low-maintenance swimming pool!"

There are all kinds of people working in real estate with the one common denominator being the high school yearbook photo that they all use in their advertising. Does your prospective agent look like Megan Fox? Expect Betty White when you actually meet her in person.

Now we all know there are some pretty sharp cookies in the real estate profession, but there is another sub-level that seems to be comprised of drifters from other lines of work. It's easy to make the switch because there are no real barriers to entry except the state real estate exam, and because "realtors" – the top of the food chain in the real estate biz – are always anxious to sign on new "agents" to do the legwork of running people around to those 129 houses with no guarantee they'll ever be paid anything for their efforts. So you run into all types of agents – housewives, college students, retired people – and a whole host of people who sell real estate as a second job. Typical conversation while your agent drives you to look for a house:

Homebuyer: Nice to meet you Mr. Real Estate Agent, have you been in real estate long?

Agent: Oh, off and on for 20 years.

Homebuyer: How did you get into it?

Agent: People just weren't throwing away as many bottles and cans as they used to and I needed to supplement my income.

All real estate agents strive to get listings because when they do, they basically have hit the mother lode. List a house and you now are the "listing agent" which means you're going to get some big bucks whenever that house sells, even if you don't sell it yourself. To get a listing, agents will promise such things as a sale within a short period of time, a better commission rate or, if need be, their first-born child. But once they get the listing, some agents become exceedingly scarce: "Oh look, dear, our listing agent just sent us a postcard from the Bahamas reminding us we owe him his commission."

The buyer's agent is pretty much the opposite – he'll be in your face right up until you sign your closing papers. That's because, of course, he won't get one thin dime until you sign your life away at closing and most of them will go to extreme lengths to make sure you don't wriggle off the hook. Expect your buyer's agent to show up at your kids' birthday parties, family funerals, major surgeries and in your bedroom as you prepare to make love to your spouse.

Homebuyer: "Oh, Mr. Buyer's Agent…you startled us…"

Agent: "Sorry to interrupt, Mrs. Jones, you go right back to what you were doing, but I just wanted to let you know that the seller has just reduced the price on the Rosecrans house and I bet we can get it for about ten grand under that… "

We had flirted with several real estate agents over the years as we got more and more serious about moving to Washington but, ironically, when we finally were ready to pull the trigger, we had no agent. Well I take that back – we had Oscar, the person who answered the phone when we called to inquire about the property that would eventually become our house.

4

Narrowing the Search

By now you're probably asking just how is it this guy can pull up and leave Southern California with no mention of a job waiting in Washington. Well that's because I have one of those jobs where I can pack my computer up and move it to another state, set it up in my new house and begin working. As my in-laws would tell you, I don't really work for a living – I run a couple of travel websites. They see me visiting wonderful places and writing about them. They don't see me sitting by my computer selling advertising, the cyber equivalent of standing on the street corner with a sign that says "Advertising for food?"

My longtime friends don't quite get it either. We once had a TV show and went to places like Austria where we would spend 18-hour days lugging equipment to ski hills and setting up dozens of shots, fighting weather and personalities to come back with the best travelogue we could. My friends just saw us on a two-week vacation in Europe, presumably getting paid for it. I half-way thought about doing one segment on West Virginia coal mines just so I could come back with grime on my face and convince them I do actually work for a living.

Our home search was done on the internet almost entirely from a distance of more than 1500 miles away. If you combine real estate websites with Google Earth, it's the next best thing to flying your own drone over Wenatchee, beaming back coordinates and high-resolution visuals of your new home. "Roger Red Dog leader, three-bedroom with office and garage sighted at 3620 River Edge Drive. Listing agent out front. Projectile armed and ready!"

The images from Google Earth are surprisingly accurate. You just find a picture of a house that you like on a real estate site and then hop over to Google Earth to see what it REALLY looks like. On the real estate site there may be more than one photo but, funny thing, they're almost always from the best angle, neatly keeping that dilapidated old garage or that 200-foot hydroelectric tower well out of view. With Google Earth, you just zoom down onto the house and fly around it, looking in every window just like you were some sort of Electronic Peeping Tom. I'm sure Google's next-generation software will have you flying right into the house, sitting down with the sellers at the dining room table or snooping through the bedrooms and rummaging through closets. "Oh, look, dear, the Google camera is back again -- make sure everyone has their clothes on!"

The real estate sites all follow a similar format which is one to 12 photos and, for the agent, a 100-word exercise in writing fiction. You can just envision the broker's semi-annual workshop teaching agents how to write their listings. "Whatever you do," the broker says, "do not reveal in any way what this house is really like. Everything in your house needs to be cute, darling, incredible or amazing. Every house will be a custom home. Every piece of property will have a sweeping view."

Of course the experienced home shopper learns to look for certain "tells" in real estate advertising, little things that give you some indication that maybe this property is not exactly a mansion in the Hamptons. The most obvious clue is when they refuse to show you a photo of the house. You read the description and it talks about a house; you look at all 12 photos and see no house. "Hmmm…this house sounds absolutely amazing and perfect for our budget, but Mr. Agent, I'm just a little hesitant here when it appears you are trying to sell me a pasture and call it a house."

If you have kids, it's important to read the fine print. For example, you want to be sure that the house you are buying is not in an Over-55 retirement community. It would be sad, indeed, for little Johnny to come back from his first foray into the neighborhood unable to really connect with friends his own age: "Dad, you told us this would be a fun new adventure and we'd meet lots of new friends, but the only friend I can find here is that guy Fred who says he likes me because I remind him of how he was when he was growing up during World War II."

Parents also will want to do their homework on the local schools and most real estate listings include some information on where your kids would be sent. The key here for most people is to go for the middle of the road. If, for example, your local high school is the Broadmoor Academy, consider

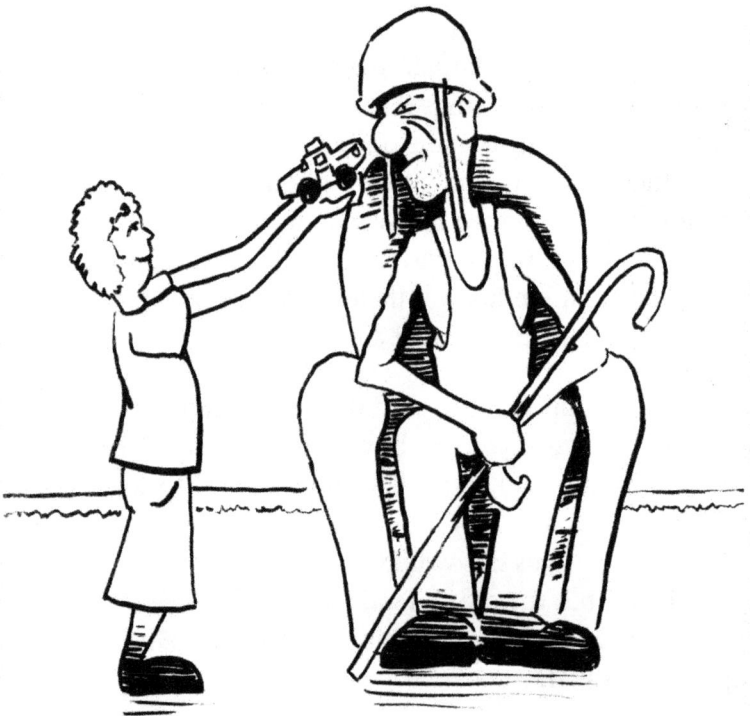

the cost of school uniforms and whether you want your kid to turn into Thurston Howell III. If, on the other hand, your kids will be going to the The Alternative School for Street Thugs, it may be best to keep looking.

We looked at houses in various neighborhoods within the city of Wenatchee but we kept thinking something was missing. Finally, it dawned on us – trees. They didn't have enough trees. They were nice houses, nice locations, but the lack of trees in Southern California had left us with an almost unquenchable thirst for trees. We had been away from trees so long that we were now obsessed with trees. The places around Wenatchee to find those trees were the forests in places like Leavenworth, Lake Chelan and certain neighborhoods near the local ski area. We expanded our search accordingly.

Now understand these places are considered the country even for people who live in the country. Wenatchee people, who arguably already live in the country, would feel like they were moving further into the country by moving to these little towns. We're talking one or two stoplights. We're talking one or two food stores. We're talking on the other side of the moon from Costco.

But sure enough, once we opened our search to the hinterlands we came upon a house that seemed to appeal to our inner Grizzly Adams – a lodge-style house with cedar shingles on a lot filled with pine trees. Jagged mountains rose from two sides, giving it that National Park feel. It was four miles from Lake Chelan, which is to North Central Washington what the Pacific Ocean is to Southern California. It was on six acres which, compared with our property in Southern California, was like moving to the Parker Ranch. All the ingredients seemed to be there.

It was time to call the listing agent. And Oscar answered the phone.

5

Dealing with Oscar

Still living in the San Diego area, we found a house in Central Washington we were interested in. We got on the phone and called the listing agent. Of course the listing agent was in the Bahamas or someplace so we talked to Oscar instead.

After a considerable amount of forensic study – okay, it was really more a gut feeling – it later became apparent to us that Oscar most likely was a custodian in the real estate office we were calling who just happened to pick up the phone the day we called. Somewhere between cleaning the toilets and taking out the trash, Oscar heard the phone ring and decided to launch his career in real estate. He was pleasant enough but when we asked for him to send us more pictures – and he didn't – we had to call back a few days later at which time another agent said she'd handle it while Oscar was in his *training* class. What did we tell you?

Now don't get us wrong. Everybody has to start someplace and we certainly wish Oscar well in his real estate career, but the feeling we were getting was like when you're wheeled into surgery for an appendectomy and the doctor is standing there with a book open to the page showing the location of the appendix. "Nurse Jones, would you hold that book up a little higher for me? I can't quite see where we should be making the incision."

It's just that rookies make mistakes and Oscar had already made his first by not following through on getting us the photos we needed. Now, remember, we were not asking him to drive us around to 129 different houses – we only wanted to see one house, and we only wanted to see it in pictures. The seasoned real estate agent who has spent years learning human behavior and effective sales techniques would call upon his vast reservoir of knowledge and realize that the next logical step was to open the file folder on his computer with the pictures, attach them to an email and send them.

Eventually, thanks to Agent B, we did get the photos but they still weren't enough to justify a couple of plane tickets to the Northwest to look at this house. So Oscar offered to go to the house and shoot some video. The plan was for him to spend some time at the house on Saturday morning shooting the various areas of the house that had not been visible on the photos. He then would upload the videos and we would view them online that afternoon. Even though our own house had not yet been sold, Oscar assured us it was likely the seller would entertain a "contingency" offer -- dependent on our home's sale – and we were anxious to move ahead quickly if this was, indeed, the right house.

Come late Saturday afternoon there were still no videos online. Checking with Oscar, he said he was still converting them to upload but couldn't get his program to work. (Translation: hang in there a little longer while I complete my real estate class on modern-day technology). By Sunday, we still didn't have videos online so we suggested another format to use for his uploading. At last, by Sunday night, we got our first look, by video, at the property in question.

Give Oscar credit, he did make a pretty thorough video taking us on a tour of every room of the house as well as on a walk around the property. He did, though, employ a rather unusual cinematic technique when shooting the mother-in-law apartment. Shooting with his iPhone he apparently figured if he turned the iPhone sideways it would somehow right itself in the final video; instead, we ended up having to turn our heads 90 degrees to view that part of the video. If you've never watched a sideways video, this is something you should try sometime. It takes extreme mental discipline to convert the sideways picture to an upright image in your own head and you'll find that repeating the exercise several times in rapid succession can actually make you slightly crazy.

What we saw on the video both encouraged and discouraged us. We could see a lot of potential in this bank-owned property, especially with its two-story fireplace and pine lodge-style interior, but the previous owner had left in a hurry with a lot of things in the house simply unfinished. The owner had actually built this home and hit hard times before completing basic elements – little things like stairs, doors, windows. The price for this three-bedroom home on six acres was in the mid $200's – dirt cheap, by California standards – but as with any bank-owned sale, the seller was not going to fix diddly-squat. What you see is what you get. And what is not working is what you have to fix. We started computing how much money we would have to spend completing the house and we soon realized that this was more than we really wanted to bite off.

Oscar, of course, had told us we could spend $5,000 and make this a $400,000 house – which made us kind of wish that Oscar was doing the appraisal for our house down in California. Suffice it to say we weren't convinced and decided to keep looking.

Until, that is, we got a call from Oscar.

6

The Offer

"I just got a call from the listing agent," Oscar said. "The bank has dropped the price by $37,000."

And so it was that a door we had pretty well shut was once again open. You can buy a lot of stairs, doors and windows for $37K and we could see that a good percentage of the improvements needed for this house could be paid for with these savings. It wouldn't cover everything we'd like to do, but maybe there were some improvements we didn't really need.

As you may know, making an offer on a house is not quite like telling your uncle George you'll give him $200 for his lawnmower. It's just not as simple as saying I have this money, you have that house and I'll swap you. If it were that simple, there would be no real estate agents, no escrow companies, no real estate attorneys and no real estate lawsuits (because there would be no real estate attorneys), and property owners would simply use frontier justice to settle their claims and disputes. The Lakota, Northern Cheyenne and Arapaho Indians used this kind of binding arbitration to great success when it was perceived that General George Armstrong Custer was claiming real estate that was not rightfully his.

And so when we told Oscar we were ready to make an offer, the next thing we knew we were engulfed in a blizzard of paperwork. Just for starters there was the financing contingency, the inspection contingency, the personal inspection contingency, utilities forms and the sale-of-our-house contingency – all in legalese, a kind of code lawyers developed long ago to make certain that people did not know what they were buying or selling. "Students, we now come to the most important part of your education here at Opaque Law School, the number one rule you must take with you for your entire career. Never, ever, ever – and we mean never – write a contract that can be understood."

We suspect this is why lawyers are so universally disliked and, as a journalist, I've often wondered if perhaps we could fix all our newspapers' financial problems by adopting the lawyers' way of doing things. We'll simply write all of our articles in code and charge the lawyers $300 an hour to tell them what we have actually written.

It was while we were preparing our offer that Oscar called with additional news. "Guess what," he said. "There is another offer on the house."

What?? Another offer?? It's funny what the second offer does to your psychology when buying a home. Right up until Oscar made that statement, we felt we were almost being coaxed into making this offer and, by golly, the bank was real lucky we were willing to come in and offer them something close to their asking price and take this quasi-dump off their hands. "Do we really want this place? Oh, I don't know, dear, it does have a lot of fixing up to do. Let's really think about this."

Thirty seconds later, with a second offer now on the table, we absolutely, positively MUST have this house or we'll regret it the rest of our lives and, what's more, our kids will regret it, and their kids will regret it and we'll feel like such fools for letting this once-in-a-lifetime opportunity pass us by. All of a sudden it's how much OVER their asking price are we going to offer? 5 grand? 10 grand? It's only money!

It's kind of like when you get a new hairstyle and you look and look and look at it in the mirror and you think to yourself, hmm, I'm really pretty hot in this new hairstyle, but then you're a little afraid to leave the house and let someone actually see you in it. But once there's one other person who sees you and agrees that you're hot, you now have been validated and are, therefore, officially hot. Well having one other person make an offer on this house validated our own inner-most thoughts. It wasn't just us! Other people could see what a great deal this was, too!

Okay, it was time to put up or shut up. We had not yet submitted our offer but the competing party's offer had been a little low – therefore, the bank asked us and the other interested buyer to each present a final and best offer. Whoever bids the highest gets the house. Very clever, those bank people, pitting us against each other like that while they get their bank vault ready to receive wads of cash from a sale they now know they cannot lose.

It was Sudden Death Playoff time. The game's tied and the refs are asking each team to attempt a field goal. The longest one wins.

Our first inclination was just to pay their full asking price. We've never paid full price for a house before and our competing buyer probably hadn't either. Therefore, full price should take it. But then I got to thinking, what if the other bidder is thinking the same thing? Okay, we'll bid $100 over the asking price. Then I got to thinking, what if the other bidder is thinking the same thing? Well these thoughts continued to volley back and forth in my head like some cerebral tennis match until finally I sat my wife down and said, you know what, we either want this house or we don't and if we do, we need to make this decisive: $5,000 over asking price. In a rare showing of complete solidarity regarding anything financial, my wife agreed with my reasoning: $5,000 over asking price it would be.

Our offer was submitted online, all documents duly signed and we awaited the results. A day later the answer came back.

"You got the house," Oscar said. "Congratulations."

"Wow, that's cool," I said, happy that we'd won but suddenly wondering if we had just been snookered into paying 5 grand more than we had to.

"Do you know what the other buyer offered?" I asked.

"Yes, I do," he said, pausing for effect. "Just $100 less than you did."

7

Inspections

Okay, we just potentially bought ourselves a house – I say "potentially" because we had not yet seen the house. Initially we'd made several trips to the Northwest to view homes -- those dark and foreboding ones in Seattle -- but soon realized we would have no money left for the house if we gave it all to the airlines. So Google Earth became our new best friend.

Yes, it's a somewhat radical way to hunt for a house – to buy it first and then look at it. We actually first thought of this when Nancy Pelosi said you have to pass the health care bill to find out what's in it. In our case, we had to buy the house to see if we wanted it. Friends did not hold back on their opinion: "I can't believe anyone would buy a house without seeing it first," one friend volunteered.

Well, in theory, we hadn't really bought the house because it would not be official until we'd signed off on the personal inspection. I had my contingency response well-rehearsed: "Oh look, there are some flies in the garage – sorry, this house will never do. My wife hates flies."

Ahead of our visit to the house, we called to line up inspectors – electrical, water, building, bugs, lousy neighbors – anything we could think of that could be a problem down the road. We'd been blissfully happy in our carefree, low-maintenance San Diego home for many years and had kind of forgotten how important it is that you stay awake during this part of the home-buying process. All of those alarms in your head should be armed and ready as you approach Inspection Day. Picture a SWAT team entering an unknown building, guns drawn, rotating in different directions trying to detect any potential threats. That's how you need to be during a home inspection.

There are inspectors, and then again there are inspectors. There are good inspectors for the buyer, and there are good inspectors for the seller. Just like an expert witness in a court of law, you can get an inspector to take a set of facts and create just about any conclusion you want him to. "Yes, the house has termites, Mr. Elliott, but that just means this house will be even stronger once we kill those little buggers off."

Now no one is going to hire an inspector and overtly tell him to lie about what he finds because, as noted in a previous chapter, there are such things as real estate attorneys, and those bad boys would just love to nail an inspector to the wall for false reporting. It's far more subtle than that and the best way to know if you have a good buyer's inspector or good seller's inspector is to follow the money.

Let's use a little logic: You're an independent home inspector who makes a living charging $400 for an hour or two of work, and your entire future – your kids' college education, your retirement savings, even the quality of rest home you one day will inhabit – depends on having a steady stream of those $400 inspections. You have on the one hand a potential home buyer who may use your services once or twice more in your lifetime. Nice to get the repeat business, but another eight hundred bucks doesn't exactly send the kids to the Ivy League, if you know what I mean.

But your other possible option is a real estate AGENCY, who could easily send you a couple more inspections THIS WEEK. If the agency is happy, you're gonna be happy, your kids are gonna be happy and, instead of living out your Golden years in a camper on Loon Lake, you'll be hosting fondue parties at your 10,000-square-foot house on the ninth green at Pebble Beach.

It's incredibly humiliating to admit this, but you probably have guessed by now that we made MISTAKE No. 1, also referred to as the Worst Possible Mistake A Homebuyer Can Make: We let the listing agency choose our inspectors. There, I've said it. I am lying on the floor, my shoe in my hand, pounding the floor over and over as I say this. I'm crying and approaching hysteria. My wife just hollered at me from the next room to turn down the TV because she does not realize I am capable of such an emotional outburst.

But once you've made a mistake of this magnitude – well, it just sticks in your gut. It's like that feeling you got back in high school when you asked a girl out for the first time in your life and she gently informed you that she would not go out with you if there were no other boys in North America and that you were so repulsive she would rather become a nun. There's a certain

sting that comes with that and there's just no getting rid of it.

As later events would play out, it became clear that this was a key juncture in this transaction, a point we think about from time to time and wonder where we would be if we had chosen our own inspectors. Kind of like going back to your wedding day and wondering how things would have turned out if you said "I don't" instead of "I do."

With the advantage of hindsight, we figure now the listing agency called up their A Team of inspectors to parachute in for a day with one objective in mind: don't screw up this sale. The sale goes through and it's Mission Accomplished. The buyer backs out and this inspection will go down in history as one of the greatest debacles since Jimmy Carter failed to rescue the hostages. "Men, you've trained for this and now the day is upon us to put that training into action. By God's grace we will persevere and let no man say from this day forward that we ever let a homebuyer escape the clutches of his real estate contract."

As you can imagine, with a real estate agent standing by as a constant reminder that Mr. Inspector will live or die based on what he puts on that inspection sheet (not dissimilar to a prisoner-of-war commandant who keeps a revolver handy for the worker who exhibits the slightest variance in camp etiquette), our house passed all the inspections with flying colors.

"You got this for WHAT price?" one of the inspectors said in an obviously rehearsed exchange just to make sure we were completely convinced that we just got the Deal of the Century. "This is exactly the kind of house I would be looking for," said another. There was no way now I was going to complain about flies in the garage – I had just pulled off a real estate HEIST. This house was such a steal we probably could sell it the day after we closed and retire on the profits!

8

Selling Our House

Back when we first considered this move, we confronted a dilemma: Do you find a house you want and then sell yours, or do you sell yours and then go shopping for a house? Like most people, we really did not want to have two house payments, so if we didn't sell our house first, we would want to buy the new house on "contingency." That means you're essentially telling the home seller: "I'll buy your house for X dollars – but then again if I don't sell my house, you can go pound sand."

In many ways it would seem more logical to sell your house first. For one thing, sellers kind of like to know their house is really sold – which means they'll do nice things for you like lower the price if they know you don't have your own house to sell.

But far be it from us to pay attention to logic. We set out on our home search knowing full well we hadn't sold our own house and realizing that only certain sellers would entertain contingency offers. This is why we were pleased when Oscar indicated the bank probably would take a contingency offer. Of course Oscar didn't know what he was talking about. When it came time to make the offer, Oscar went back to the bank and the conversation went something like this:

Oscar: My buyers are ready to make that contingency offer now.

The Bank: What contingency offer? Are you crazy?

Oscar: But..uh…I thought…

The Bank: How dare you sniveling little punk agent come to the Great Bank of Everything Good and suggest that we sell one of our properties on CONTINGENCY! We the Magnificent Benefactors of the Universe did not amass our great fortune by selling houses on contingency!

Fortunately it was just about this time that we did, in fact, sell our house. I had sent an email to friends mentioning the house was going up for sale and that now was the time to buy it without paying a real estate commission. If there is one universal thought or feeling out there it is that a real estate agent should never get a commission and that basically they were put on this earth for one purpose, and one purpose only: to drive us around to look at houses. Bingo! A friend of a friend called and wanted to look at the house.

Now let me tell you we had been preparing for this moment for years. We knew at some point we were going to have to sell our house in order to go back to Washington, and all we'd been reading about was how tough it was to sell a house since the Great Real Estate Screw-up of 2008. We really wondered just how much we were going to get out of this house because of a disappointing appraisal done on the house about a year before.

Appraisers, if you didn't know, are highly skilled professionals trained to do one thing: Convince you that your house is worth absolutely nothing. They do this through a complex algorithm that averages the price paid for three homes in your neighborhood and then multiplies that by 1/10 of one percent, producing a final number that usually ends up being less than you paid for pizza last Friday night. "Sorry, Mr. Elliott, I tried to add a little extra for your custom chrome-plated dog house, but the market right now just won't support a higher price."

Back before 2008, we and our Southern California neighbors were just sitting back, watching the home prices go up, up and up, mentally theorizing that we could, in fact, retire on a Greek island if we just let things roll for another few years. I'd get together with the boys in the neighborhood to watch football and the conversation would always come around to our houses which we viewed pretty much as gold mining operations that did not require the hassle of actually extracting the gold.

Football Buddy 1: Hey, how's your house doin'?

Football Buddy 2: Terrific, dude – probably worth about 800K now.

Football Buddy 3: Nah, these houses are over a million now.

Football Buddy 1: No way, guys, they're at least a million two – that's what my wife said, anyway, when she talked me into the matching his-and-her BMW's.

Of course, then along came 2008, and soup lines started forming in our cul-de-sac – well maybe that's an exaggeration but the mood definitely soured as we all came to grips with the notion that we were not, in fact, headed for a blissful retirement in Greece and were more likely to spend our Golden years greeting customers at the local Walmart. The phrase "'Til death do us part" no longer had anything to do with marriage – it now described our employment agreements.

So it was against this backdrop that our prospective buyers came by to look at our house. We had a year-old appraisal that basically said the house was worthless, we were beaten down by all the bad news about the economy and we were almost ready to pay the buyers to take the house off our hands. We greeted this pleasant couple and their agent at the door and then showed them the house. At the conclusion of the showing we sat down with them at the dining room table and expected the usual barrage of questions and complaints designed to wear us down even further.

But a funny thing happened on the way to the table. The buyers – who already knew our asking price – were ready to buy. Full price. Their agent had brought the necessary paperwork and, before we could say "do you wanna buy the house?" they had already bought it.

Now you have to understand the sales dynamic here and, for those of you not in sales, I'll try to put it in layman's terms. Suppose you're a used car salesman and you make your living by gently persuading customers to buy vehicles they really didn't need or want before they came onto your lot. The sale of our house was the equivalent of a customer forcing a used car dealer to sell a car to him. "I'll give you $10,000 for that '89 Buick over there – and not a penny less!"

We had been so conditioned to expect absolutely nothing for our house that the first thought that came to my mind was: What do they know that we don't know? Has someone discovered oil on our property? Has someone started digging for diamonds in those backyard holes that we thought had been dug by our dog? The next thought was maybe these WERE million-dollar houses after all -- and now it would be the new buyers who would be retiring on our Greek island.

9

The Financing

With our house sold, it was now easier to buy the new house in the Northwest -- but someone forgot to tell our lender that. Oh, they knew we sold our house all right, but that wasn't going to stop them from making us go through Boot Camp for Homebuyers, a process where they strip you down to the essence of your humanity and finally bring you to the belief, over a series of days and weeks, that you truly cannot afford and do not deserve the house you just bought.

It all starts innocently enough with the incessant radio commercials that your lender uses to bombard you with the revelation that money for your house is waiting for you, with your name on it, tied up with a bow, and all you need to do is call and they'll give you all the money you would ever need. In fact, there's no real reason to work for a living because this lender will just GIVE you money. Interest rates? They seem to go lower with every new 30-second commercial – 3 percent, 2.5 percent, 1 percent, oh heck forget about interest because we're so magnanimous we're just going to give you the money as our way of helping stamp out poverty.

When you call the lender they're all excited to hear from you because you know the one thing in this life they like to do is give away money. If you ask what's required to get your home loan, you're likely to get their stock answer: "All I need, Mr. Elliott, is about 10 minutes of your time on the telephone and we can get you pre-approved." Whoa – that sounds great. In less time than it takes me to order a pizza, I will have buku bucks ready to plunk down on my new house. I can't believe what wonderful people those lenders are and I must remember to repay my loan officer in my will for his kindness.

The only problem is that pre-approval is not approval, a nasty little detail that does not at first seem obvious when you're still in the afterglow of all those promises of free money.

The idea behind a pre-approval is that it theoretically helps a buyer know how much he can afford to pay for a house, and it helps the seller know that the buyer isn't really on public assistance just making offers on houses for fun. When the lender gives you a pre-approval letter, you just take that with you when you're ready to make an offer and it's like telling everyone you're a member of the club. "Ahem, Mr. Real Estate agent, I have right here in my possession this official authorization from Do-gooder Bank to buy any house I desire, and I will thank you, in the future, Mr. Real Estate Agent, not to question my financial veracity."

Except that a pre-approval letter isn't really worth the paper it's printed on. All you have to do is read the fine print at the bottom of the letter: "Nothing in the language used in this pre-approval letter is meant to construe to said seller that said buyer actually has said funds to actually buy said house and if you agree to sell said house to said buyer you're an idiot."

The reality is a pre-approval letter is kind of a temporary learner's permit like when you're just learning how to drive. It allows you to get in the game but you still really can't do anything unless someone else is there to hand over the money. To get your full "license" you're going to have to maneuver through a series of obstacles your lender has put in place to make sure you're not a financial menace to society.

It all starts with the paperwork the lender requests. Income tax returns are at the top of the list which is problematic for a lot of people who have completed such forms with a careful eye toward minimizing their income since the object of the game is to not exactly brag to Uncle Sam about how much money you make. But when it comes time to submit these to a lender, those chickens finally come home to roost: "We see here, Mr. Jones, you show earned income of $8,735 for the previous calendar year and yet you are proposing to spend approximately 100 times that on your new house. Do you realize we will have to write this loan for a term of 275 years in order for you to afford your monthly payments?"

And that's just the beginning. Your lender will then probe every aspect of your life, asking you to justify every penny that was spent out of your bank account. "Mr. Jones, we see that on April 23, 2013 you bought a Big Whopper at the Burger King in Escondido, California. Can you tell us whether you had fries with that?"

The list of records you have to submit is worse than applying for political asylum in Kyrgyzstan. "Please submit all bank records, school records, hospital records, arrest records, any documentation of past extra-marital affairs, a dossier on all in-house pets and the password to your Facebook account."

What the lender does with this information is anyone's guess but the one thing they won't do until approximately 48 hours before your closing is actually work on your loan. This is known as the "48 Hour Rule" and is the first thing they teach on the first day of Lending School. "Now, class, some of you may have developed the bad habit of being organized but success in our profession is directly proportionate to the amount of chaos you can create in your borrowers' lives. Therefore, it is a strict tenet of the Professional Lenders Code that you must always procrastinate and you must never, ever fund a loan when you say you will."

We dutifully submitted our paperwork and, of course, believed our lender when they said they'd have the whole thing wrapped up and funded within 30 days. We innocently went on about the business of selling our house and moving out while, lurking just over the horizon, was the Monster of Future Real Estate Chaos just waiting to swoop down and crush our dream of moving to the country.

10

Preparing for the Move

While our loan application sat in somebody's bottom desk drawer waiting out the 48 Hour Rule, we began our preparations for the move from California to the Pacific Northwest. After 14 years in the same house, we were about to explore one of the World's greatest frontiers – right up there with space and the oceans – where we would discover unknown creatures and forgotten resources tucked far away from public view. We were about to pry open our storage closets.

But before we could proceed, we had to get some logistical support. Like the D-Day Invasion at Normandy, you couldn't just wave a wand and have everything just magically appear at the new destination. This was going to take planning and careful foresight, and just like Eisenhower called in his top generals to figure out how to move men and materiel vast distances, we called in our own go-to expert on moving to a new house: my sister-in-law, Barb.

This was actually the second time we had brought her in for this kind of a mission – she had helped us move to California 14 years earlier. Everyone was put on this earth with a special talent and my sister-in-law seems to have inherited some sort of special gene for packing. She has the uncanny ability to pack 30 cubic feet of cargo into a 20 cubic-foot container. She also can lift twice her weight, rarely complains and works for free, all qualities you want to look for when choosing someone of good stock to help you move your household belongings.

We had priced a moving company and quickly rejected the many thousands of dollars that would have added to our cost of moving. We checked on moving truck rentals and found we could rent the Mother of All Moving Trucks for about $1500 one way. We reserved the truck several weeks in advance and then began to gradually inventory our belongings and prepare them for transit.

The plan was for Barb to show up the last week before D-Day and, in the meantime, my wife and I would get started on packing things up. But with about four weeks until D-Day my wife did not yet feel enough pressure to actually let me help her pack. Maybe she thought I was completely incompetent at packing or maybe she wanted to have complete control over the process, but every time I volunteered to pack up a few things she sent me to my bedroom closet with strict instructions to pack up my own clothes and to not go one step further. Okay, I thought, who am I to argue with making her do all the work? She did not have to twist my arm to spend a little more time watching football and drinking beer with the boys.

Of course there's no such thing as a free lunch, and there is no such thing as shirking your responsibilities in a marriage without some sort of eventual punishment, even if your wife practically draws you a diagram explaining how to goof off. It was just about D-Day minus 10 days when it dawned on me we weren't going to make it – we weren't going to get everything packed in time. The feeling can best be described by picturing that scene in Titanic where one of the crewmembers spots the iceberg through his binoculars and then gets this expression on his face like he's about to give birth to a basketball and he begins clanging the bell so hard it nearly falls off the bridge. I had seen the iceberg -- so I began clanging the bell.

Clanging the bell in this instance meant venturing beyond my restricted air space and packing items that were not in my closet. I hurriedly began dumping books, papers, trinkets, electronics, pets, you-name-it into huge boxes, hoping that my wife was so busy with her own packing that she would not notice my rank insubordination. It soon became apparent, however, that my wife also had seen the iceberg. Unofficially at least she lifted my restrictions and tried not to grimace as I proceeded to demonstrate my true talent for quickly dumping as much stuff in as many boxes as possible.

Barb, meanwhile, had arrived on scene and had begun her methodical, meticulous, step-by-step packing that involved cutting the proper size wrapping paper for each item, wrapping said item, and placing it into a custom box. She manufactured her custom boxes by cutting a piece of cardboard to exacting specifications and folding the cardboard so that the box was not in the shape of a box, but rather in the shape of the item. Then the custom boxes were grouped with other boxes and put into a larger box where one day future archeologists would open these larger boxes and figure the only

thing that could possibly have been dissembled and packaged with such care was the Lost Ark of the Covenant. Oh to see their faces when they open everything up to find individually wrapped cassette tapes from the The Greatest Metal Bands of the 1980's.

With hindsight there are a few things we might have done differently. First, Barb's method of packing made for an extremely efficient use of space but it also meant that, in all likelihood, we'd never see the items in these boxes again. When you have a garage full of these boxes – the scene in Raiders of the Lost Ark comes to mind, the one where there are acres and acres of boxes and antiquities stored in the warehouse – it's really hard to remember where anything is. "Honey, I can't remember where we packed the popcorn machine – guess we'll have to buy a new one!"

Labeling the boxes may help but be sure you label the boxes on every side. We, of course, labeled them on one side, meaning when you're in that Raiders of the Lost Ark warehouse looking for something, you have to pick up every box that does not happen to have the label side facing out. "Dear, I need to set aside four hours this afternoon to move every box in the garage so that I can find my mustache trimmer."

It was during our packing that we also discovered something else: The U-Haul Quantum Theory of Boxes Needed versus Boxes Actually Purchased. This law of nature dictates that the need for moving boxes grows in direct proportion to the time spent packing boxes, meaning quite simply you will never, ever have enough boxes. Scientists theorize that, just like sub-atomic particles, these boxes buzz around each other, colliding and bonding, and then eventually they fall into one great big cosmic Black Hole requiring you to go back to U-Haul and plunk down another 3 bucks per box. This means, of course, the Mother of All Moving Trucks now comes with the Mother of All Visa Card Charges to pay for this unending stream of boxes.

It's also during a move that you start to realize there are certain differences in the way people view the belongings they have accumulated over an adult lifetime. In fact, we think newlyweds should be given a Storage Compatibility Test to be sure there is no undue friction later in their marriage. The problem is that there are basically two kinds of people – the kind that likes to accumulate stuff throughout their marriage, and the kind that can't stand to look at the stuff accumulated throughout their marriage.

It's basically the hoarders versus the cleaners. The hoarders cannot release an item from their possession because someday they may be able to use it again, or at the very least they can sell it on E-Bay. "Don't throw away that Hibachi! Yes, I know we now have a six-burner gas grill and yes I know that the Hibachi weighs so much it will qualify for its own FedEx truck if we ever have to ship it to a buyer, but you just never know if someday our kids might want to use it -- or maybe we can use it as a planter!"

On the other end of the spectrum are the cleaners, whose life mission is to have a garage floor so clean they can have the grandchildren lick their bubblegum off it. These are the people who have the garage that looks like a new car showroom with walls, cabinets and floors gleaming and not a storage box or tool in sight. My father-in-law is a cleaner. Whenever he looks at our garage – which often has a certain junkyard motif – he suggests we just shovel all the stuff down to the curb and put a big "free" sign on it so people will come and take it all away.

I must say I may have a little bit of cleaner in me because, after decades of storing stuff we never, ever will use in three lifetimes, I am starting to see my father-in-law's reasoning. Another factor in my transformation is that we have been paying storage fees on items we could not live without but have never seen again since we put them in storage 14 years ago.

In many ways my wife is a cleaner too – she definitely detests a messy house – but she can't bring herself to follow her father's advice. She wants to take the time to sort through every item and, of course, the problem with that is she would be forfeiting a wonderful retirement full of kissing grandkids and cavorting with church friends to spend her remaining days on this earth pawing through a never-ending pile of refuse.

So the net result is we just kick the can on down the road or, in this case, move the boxes on down the road to another storage facility or another garage where they will sit until one day a future explorer will think he's discovered a King Tut's Tomb full of Hibachis, bread machines and old fishing poles – a revealing glimpse into American life as it once existed in the 21st Century.

11

The Moving Guys

I don't know about you but the older I get the less inclined I am to lift ANY-thing. Oh I might lift the occasional case of beer, but anything heavier than that, forget about it. That's because I've had a couple of brushes with sciatica, which is Nature's way of reminding you that you were born with an expiration date. Sciatica produces excruciating back pain and it has something to do with nerves rubbing against vertebrae or vice versa. All I know is that, once it kicks in, you cannot move 1/8 inch in any direction without a huge burst of pain. It gets so bad you actually weigh the pros and cons of getting up to go to the bathroom.

So the last thing I was going to do was move my own household belongings. Once all those boxes were packed it would be time to bring in the young bucks who do this sort of thing for a living. You just wind them up and let them go.

We did a little calling around and found a local company that hires out movers by the hour. They show up with a truck and will move you around town or wherever. In our case, we had the Mother of All Moving Trucks so all they had to do was show up with their bodies and pack our truck. We placed our order and sat back, waiting for Hulk Hogan and Arnold Schwarzenegger to arrive. At the appointed time, in walked Don Knotts and Peewee Herman.

I'm thinking to myself, how are these two wimpy little guys going to move approximately 15 tons of Elliott family history? Are there laws on the books against cruelty to movers? What's the game here – they try to lift one of our boxes, fall down the stairs, sue us for everything we own and six months from now we're helping THEM move into OUR house?

Well, I needn't have worried. It was amazing the heavy stuff they would pile onto their backs and hustle out to the truck. Washer-dryer? No problem.

Stand-alone freezer? No sweat. Big solid oak desk? Piece of cake. Whatever we threw at them they just WILLED it onto the truck as we stood nearby, hoping neighbors wouldn't see us loading them down like they were Sherpas headed for Mount Everest and turn us in for unfair labor practices.

And talk about packers. They were like my sister-in-law Barb on steroids. I think they could see from the moment they pulled into our driveway that we had roughly two trucks of belongings to pile into just one truck, and that their only hope was to use every cubic inch of space, top to bottom, wedging things in so tightly you would need an earthquake to shake it all loose again. It was not their fault that what we really needed was a FLEET of moving trucks to haul every last Hibachi, bread machine and old fishing pole to their new place of storage.

When all was said and done, we had made our deadline. The truck was filled to the brim and our two cars were packed with household belongings like an updated version of the Beverly Hillbillies. My son-in-law flew in from his home in the Northwest to gallantly drive the Mother of All Moving Trucks the 1500 miles to our new home in North Central Washington. My wife and I drove our two cars. San Diego was now in our rear-view mirror and we had begun a three-day journey northward.

Meanwhile, somewhere in Lender Land, our loan application still sat in someone's bottom desk drawer waiting out the 48-hour rule. And soon we would be officially homeless.

12

The Journey North

So far, so good – we were loaded up and on the road. Our entire lives had been packed into these three vehicles that now made their way through Southern California headed for the magical destination of Chowchilla, the end of our first leg of this journey where we would spend the night at a hotel.

As we proceeded north, we thought about the memories we were leaving behind – the friends we would see much less frequently now, the incredibly comfortable San Diego weather and, as it turned out, all sense of normalcy. There had been a certain structure and predictability that we could count on living in our house in San Diego and we had now put our fate in the hands of our lender and real estate agents, assuming rather naively that everyone would do their job on time and that, in just days, we would be moved into our new home in North Central Washington.

Meanwhile, somewhere out there in Lender Land in an office cubicle far, far away, there was a loan officer chuckling to herself about the havoc she would soon wreak on the unsuspecting Elliotts. The Wicked Loan Officer of the West was laughing almost uncontrollably as she stared into her crystal ball at the innocent Elliotts driving north on Interstate 5: "I'll get you my little pretty...ha ha ha ha...and your little dog, too! Ha ha ha ha..."

Of course we had no idea this was happening. We had carefully planned the sale of our house and the purchase of the new house to happen in a logical order, all in time for us to move our belongings into the new house shortly after arrival. We signed the papers selling our house before we left town, and our eager buyers – the ones who will someday be selling our house for a million bucks – were more than happy to get us our money quickly.

On the other hand, our lender had not yet completely approved our loan. We were heading north on a wing and a prayer and a "pre-approval" that wasn't worth the paper it was written on. Yes, we did have the assurance of our loan officer that all was well and she expected the loan to be funded by the time we ended our three-day journey to the new house. But that and $3.50 would barely buy us a cup of Starbucks coffee.

The first day was uneventful as we pulled into our waypoint for the night with some confidence that all was going according to plan. My son-in-law had determined that the Mother of All Moving Trucks had some problem negotiating steep grades and so, to compensate for the 45 miles per hour he would have to drive when going uphill, he would drive it 90 miles an hour downhill. He had brought a couple of our young grandsons and both boys, despite having a long history of conquering every challenging roller-coaster on the West Coast, were discernibly pale and non-talkative when they climbed down from the truck after their first day on the road.

The second day would involve more challenges. Headed for Klamath Falls, Oregon, we caravanned up Interstate 5 for a few miles but, at 90 miles an hour, my son-in-law John quickly pulled into the lead and eventually got as far as 70 miles ahead of us when he gave us a call on the cell phone:

John: I was just pulled over.

Me: What? I told you not to drive so fast.

John: No, they say I weigh too much.

Me: I told you to go on that diet.

John: No, the truck weighs too much. They say I have to remove 1400 pounds!

Okay, this is where the Great Move to the Northwest seriously started to go off script. No one had anticipated that there was actually a weight limit for the Mother of All Moving Trucks. It was just so big, the assumption was you could put an aircraft carrier on top of it and, while the tires might be a little taxed, the truck could handle the weight just fine.

As it turns out, John had seen a sign that said all trucks must exit the interstate to be weighed at the truck scales and he dutifully pulled in to have the truck weighed. Next thing he knows a state patrol officer is impounding the truck until he can remove 1400 pounds of cargo.

Picture having to leave 1400 pounds of your most precious lifetime memories out in the middle of the wilderness, scattering bread machines and Hibachis through the forest in an attempt to make them at least look like they are bio-degradable. Picture Smokey the Bear with his official wide-brimmed hat, aviator glasses and bow tie, tapping his foot while you determine just how you're going to dispose of 1400 pounds without getting a ticket for littering.

One can only wonder what John would have done had he been traveling alone with no other vehicles trailing him, but the solution was that we would shift the extra weight to one of us. To do that, we had to rent a U-Haul trailer for the rest of the trip to Washington state. Fortunately there was a rental facility between us and John and a couple hours later we caught up with my son-in-law and began off-loading the offending tonnage. Unfortunately, the trailer would cost almost as much as the Mother of All Moving Trucks.

It was an inconvenient, costly and frustrating delay but just a few hours behind schedule we arrived at Klamath Falls ready to bed down for our second night on the road. Just one more day on the road to our destination and our new house would close a day or two after that. This all would be over in a couple of days – or would it?

Funny, but we hadn't yet heard anything from our lender. We'd left numerous messages but now, as we entered one of the most crucial phases of the operation, it was radio silence. Was it just us, or was there truly something to be worried about?

13

Hostage Crisis

It was just a day's drive to our destination near Wenatchee, Washington and we woke up that Wednesday in Klamath Falls, Oregon, excited that we were almost home. The plan was to spend a couple of nights at my inlaws' house, sign the final closing papers on our new house and move in on Friday. Weeks before, we had already lined up movers to be on site and ready to unload our truck.

When our caravan pulled into my inlaws' driveway, there was a certain sense of accomplishment as well as relief that no further mishaps had occurred along the way. We were bearing one more U-Haul trailer than originally planned but, what the heck, we figured if that was the worst of our problems we were okay. Everyone was healthy, no vehicles were harmed and the Mother of All Moving Trucks had not broken down even when subjected to our son-in-law's version of the Baja 1000.

But as relieved as we felt about finally getting to our destination, there was a gnawing feeling somewhere in the back of my mind that something was not quite right. The listing agent was all ready to turn over the keys to the new house but he was insisting that we actually pay for the house first. That required that we get money from our lender and, thus far, we weren't even getting phone calls from our lender. What was wrong with this picture?

When Friday came and still there was no funding from our lender, it was time to call off the movers – there would be no move-in that day and, in fact, that day would become Day 1 of our own drawn-out Hostage Crisis. For it was on that day that we realized we had absolutely no place to unload our household belongings – they were being held hostage on our rental truck until we could close the sale of our new house.

Now put yourself in our shoes: We had everything from furniture to tooth brushes in a moving truck so tightly packed that you would need an ultrasound to find something buried underneath the rubble. In three days we'd gone from having everything we needed at our comfortable sun-drenched Southern California home to living out of a suitcase in my inlaws' tiny downstairs apartment. We were babysitting a rental truck that was costing us $50 for every day we could not unload it.

To make matters worse, we had also scheduled some major remodeling to start on the new house and had gone so far as to have a contractor friend of ours drive from California and be ready to begin work on the new house on the day it was originally scheduled to close.

So let's review:

1 We're sitting in my inlaws' Washington driveway with a packed moving truck we cannot unload because we can't get into our new house.

2 We're traveling not only with our family of three, but now have a "crew" that includes my sister-in-law the packer and our contractor friend who actually expects to begin work on the new house that we cannot even get into.

3 All progress toward closing our new house depends on our lender who is now on the dark side of the moon and out of radio communication for the foreseeable future.

Thus began a kind of siege where we all hunkered down at my inlaws' house, wearing the same clothes every day, emailing our lender each day and leaving phone messages, hoping that we could bring our Hostage Crisis to a peaceful conclusion. We would pass the time by playing dominos and dreaming of life on the outside when one day we would all get our lives back and look back and joke about our time in detention. Every day started looking just like the day before it and we would lose track of time to the extent that we started drawing marks on my inlaws' wall to count the days in captivity: One, two, three, four days, and then a mark diagonally across those marks to round it off to five. Neighbors were putting yellow ribbons on our moving truck.

Paul, our contractor friend, would every once in awhile pull out a power drill and just rev it up to make sure it was still working and to remind him of what his former life used to be like. On especially bleak days, he would put on his tool belt. My sister-in-law Barb would pack and repack boxes just to make sure she still had her mental acuity.

On about Day 8 of the Hostage Crisis, we did finally talk to a live person at the lending company. In what felt like a breakthrough at the time, this person told us he would talk to our loan officer and have her get back to us. But alas, more days went by without any contact and this left us feeling like the survivors in a lifeboat who spotted a rescue ship that just kept sailing over the horizon.

Several more days passed until, nearly two weeks into the crisis, we suddenly got our loan paperwork to sign. No particular explanation why it was late. No sorry for the delay, no thank you for bearing with us while we made you sweat bullets, no offer to pay $700 in late charges we had incurred on the Mother of All Moving Trucks. To the lender, it was just business as usual.

Those of you paying close attention will recognize that the real problem here had been the 48 Hour Rule. To recap, that is the rule that requires lenders to leave your loan paperwork in their bottom desk drawer until 48 hours before the scheduled closing date. From the lender's perspective there was no sense in calling if they hadn't even looked at our paperwork. From our perspective, our lender had fallen off the face of the earth.

But the crisis was over now and we were just relieved that they were back in communication and writing checks. After all this, there was one thing we knew for sure: Being homeless really isn't all it's cracked up to be.

14

Offloading

The Hostage Crisis had gone on so long that, by the time we could offload our belongings into the new house, our original movers had turned into flakes. By that I mean the pleasant, professional, even obsequious man who had been calling me a couple times each week to assure me his crew would be ready when the house was ready – was no longer ready. He, like the lender, just seemed to vanish. We arranged to meet him at the new house on moving day and he just didn't bother to show up.

Hmmm. We were beginning to wonder what the moving gods had against us. Nothing, it seemed, was going smoothly in our move to the country. What to do now?

By chance we stumbled upon a storefront in Wenatchee that appeared to offer temporary labor of the type that we were now desperately seeking. The only problem was that Paul and I had noticed a couple of grungy guys nearby who looked like they were on their way to see their parole officer. "I don't know, Paul, we need the help unloading, but do we really want those guys to have the opportunity to do a detailed inventory of our household belongings?" Don't worry about it, Paul assured me, those are just street people – they use other people to hire out.

Fifteen minutes later the paperwork was finished, the Visa card swiped, and the temporary employment agency manager took us back out to the street to meet the two shadowy figures we had just been talking about. "Meet your new employees, Mr. Elliott!"

Things were moving very quickly now as we drove back to our new house, leading our new shady character friends right to our doorstep. The move-in today would afford our new friends an excellent opportunity to diagram our floor plan, including all areas for ingress and egress and the best route to use for a fast getaway. The only thing they would be missing would be a key to the house, but the move-in would give them ample time to figure out which windows to smash.

We brought in the Mother of All Moving Trucks, a little concerned that it might sink into our dirt driveway never to be recovered. Fortunately the driveway held up and we carefully backed the truck as close as possible to the garage to begin offloading boxes. This garage, by the way, will probably never again actually house a vehicle. More likely it will become a permanent storage unit for the boxes of "must-have" belongings that our kids will have to clean out once we're on the way to the nursing home.

The shady characters were picking up steam now, anxious no doubt to see what loot was still hidden in the truck. We surmised it must have seemed like a treasure hunt to them – one minute they're doing doobies in the street comparing notes about which penitentiary had the best yoga class, and the next they're on a shopping spree picking out which high-value items they were going to plunder in the easiest caper they'd had since they were kids pocketing bubble gum.

But then something strange happened. We began to get the sense that maybe these guys were actually honest workers, or at least that they were saying and doing the right things. We got to talking with them as they huffed and puffed, grunted and groaned and carried amazingly heavy pieces of furniture into our house and it started to feel like they were really in this to earn an honest buck. They worked tirelessly, anxious to do a good job and they carefully followed all of our instructions. Our pre-conceptions began to melt away and we now felt guilty we had judged them by their appearance.

By dusk, the job was done and we rewarded our new friends with a generous tip. Maybe we had just lived in the Big City too long where you tend to err on the side of suspicion and are always cautious when forming new relationships. There just might be a different set of rules out in the country where people are happy to give you a friendly wave for doing nothing more than driving past them on the highway.

15

Bomb Damage Assessment

BDA is short for Bomb Damage Assessment and it's when the military goes back after a strike to figure out just how much damage was done. The same principle applies in real estate when you buy a house from a bank that has put in the sales contract roughly 37 times that they are selling you the house "as is" and that Hell will freeze over before they spend any money fixing any issues with this house. After using inspectors who may as well have been wearing blindfolds, there was every possibility we had actually bought a neighborhood crack house only momentarily disguised as the charming mountain home we thought we had purchased.

So the first order of business was to conduct a comprehensive BDA of the property -- to get a true picture of the home's condition. Okay, we weren't looking at a bombed-out hulk, but we did notice right away a few problems such as the upstairs carpet torn out, doors and windows missing or mismatched, electrical systems that didn't work, a stairway that was incomplete, railings missing, a water system that didn't work and a couple of doors that apparently bore the scratches of a very impatient dog.

It was ironic that we were even in this position. Early in our house hunt, I set down my conditions for moving to the Northwest, explaining to my wife that the last thing on earth I wanted was a fixer-upper that required some sort of mechanical know-how to fix. I was flexible on a lot of things, but the condition of the house was not one of them. So of course we bought a fixer-upper.

My close friends will understand why I drew this line in the sand because they're the ones who have observed me over the years as I tried to tackle simple household improvements only to end up hiring a professional repairman or worse, have my wife do it. This latter option was pretty much the equivalent of grabbing a lifeboat and leaving my wife to perish on the

Titanic and, quite frankly, is embarrassing to admit. But as an MMGAB, I had little choice.

I first knew I might be an MMGAB (Missing Mechanical Gene At Birth) when our 7th grade curriculum required all boys to take shop while the girls took home economics. Since my dad probably was MMGAB as well, I'd never been exposed to a world of lathes, power sanders and table saws, and naturally assumed that such things as book cases, end tables and cabinets were created by God and more or less harvested fully assembled in some sort of furniture plantation in the Deep South. All of a sudden here I was in this class that required me to make pieces of furniture out of plain pieces of wood. Maybe Jesus could make something out of nothing, but I was pretty sure I couldn't.

And I was right. I look back now at the remarkable patience my shop teacher had with me when he inspected my first effort to power sand my birch end table and found that I had created a depression in this board deep enough to hold a gallon of water. Now he could have made matters worse: "Hey everybody look over here at what Mr. Elliott has done! What an idiot! Don't any of you do this or I will flunk your rear-ends right out of this class!" But fortunately for me he was more discreet (obviously sensing he was dealing here with an MMGAB) and he just kind of whispered to me that it might be best to start over.

This process repeated itself in various ways throughout the course of that long school year and while most of my classmates were producing furniture like it was coming down some sort of factory conveyer belt, I turned in a grand total of two completed items and skated by with a C only made possible by my teacher's self-delusion that perhaps I would find my inner builder later in life. Well, it's now later in life and, unfortunately, my teacher had much more faith in my abilities than I deserved.

I did make one valiant effort in my mid-twenties to buck up and build like a man. For some reason I got the notion that we needed a house for our cat and, while I had a little time at home alone, I ventured out into the garage looking for tools I almost didn't recognize because I hadn't been around them since 7th grade. I gathered up everything I thought I needed and carefully measured my wood, refusing to follow any sort of plan because I knew in my head how I wanted it to look. Many hours later I presented the fin-

ished product to my wife who immediately pronounced it uninhabitable –
even for a cat.

Interestingly, I don't have the same disability when I work with computers
or electronics, so a DNA sample probably would show I am only missing
half the mechanical gene, which gives me hope that someday there may be
a restorative cure. "Doctor, your patient, Mr. Elliott, just awakened from his
gene surgery and the operation was a success – the first thing he asked for
was a power drill!"

But until such a cure is found, I likely will have problems fixing up my fixer-
upper. This was the rationale behind bringing in Paul, the contractor. A West
Virginia native with a smooth southern drawl, Paul conveys the image of
someone who is confident in his mechanical skills and willing to try just
about anything the client wants. Fit and trim in his jeans, tool belt and hard
hat, Paul not only looks like one of the Village People, but he plays guitar and
sings as well. This came in handy during the Hostage Crisis when he broke
the boredom of daily dominoes with live performances in my inlaws' small
apartment. It was almost like we had our own visiting USO Tour.

On his first visit to our new house, Paul displayed a remarkably good bedside manner as he explained to us, much the way a doctor would tell you that
you have a terminal illness, that our house was very sick and needed radical
surgery for any chance at a meaningful life. He didn't say we had to burn
down the house and start over, but it seemed like it came pretty close to that.
The Deal of the Century apparently had been made by the bank, not by us,
and it was going to take thousands of dollars to fix the problems.

This probably explained why we had not heard from Oscar our real estate
agent ever since the day we closed the deal. Who knows, he may have tried
the business out just long enough to make this one sale and then gone back
to his janitorial duties. Come to think of it, there were no housewarming
parties being thrown by our inspectors either. "Welcome to your new house,
Mr. Elliott – we're sure you'll spend many happy years rebuilding all the
things that we didn't tell you needed rebuilding!"

Of course no problem is so great that it can't be overcome by a credit card, so
one of the first things we did was to leave a credit card down at two different
local hardware stores. This was so Paul could go on a shopping spree any-

time without worrying about the cost. We couldn't help but feel like parents giving our kid the keys to the family car: "Here you go, Paul – take this and prove to us that you can be responsible for your actions. If not we'll have to take it away!"

But that was just the beginning. Before our project was finished, we would earn a degree in big-box hardware stores and have the distinct feeling that we had bought enough merchandise to own a small percentage of both Lowe's and Home Depot.

16

The Work Begins

We were moved into our new house but only in the sense that we had piled all our moving boxes into the garage where most of them would remain unopened for approximately the next two decades. We were now entering the remodel phase of our move to the country – that period when it finally dawns on you that buying a cheap house is not going to be cheap.

Among other things, the house would require new floors so it wasn't practical for us to actually move in and start living in the new house. But the house did have a mother-in-law apartment that had a relatively good BDA and was a good place for Paul the contractor to settle in and enjoy our new house. Paul would be the test pilot, trying out the house for us as we commuted from the inlaws' house 23 miles away.

We have to give Paul a lot of credit here for that first night he spent alone in our house. It was a little like a TV episode of Ghost Adventures where they choose a haunted building to lock themselves in for an overnight stay and spend the night deluding themselves into thinking they are seeing ghosts. Sure enough, Paul heard noises he couldn't explain and all he could think about was the home's previous owner coming back to murder the new owner's contractor. He had a sidearm always at his bedside which turned out to be a little scary for everyone on the third night when we came up to visit and barged in on a sleeping Paul. "Here lay the Elliott family, may they rest in peace – their only regret was that they did not live to see the completion of their remodel."

The house we had just purchased was almost an hour's drive to the nearest Lowe's or Home Depot, but that was a minor speed bump on our way to transferring a substantial portion of our wealth to local home improvement stores. It was bad enough writing the checks but Paul was so busy remodeling that he sent us on regular runs to these stores where we could see up-close and personal how our kid's college fund was slowly evaporating with the purchase of every board, tile, molding, bracket, nail and screw. Our carpet cost approximately half as much as our first house. The hardwood flooring obviously was made of compacted gold dust, the only explanation we could think of for the price.

And, in some ways, it was like Shop Class all over again. Every time Paul would give us a list of building materials he needed it was as though the list was in a foreign language. Sometimes we could kinda, sorta make out what he was talking about, but lots of times we had no clue. All-purpose joint compound, for example, was something we really expected to find at Walgreens Pharmacy.

The only people more clueless, though, were some of the employees at the home improvement stores. Near as we can tell, these stores use two different job descriptions when hiring new employees:

Job Description 1: Local home improvement store seeks experienced, industrious and knowledgeable worker to offer intelligent answers to people seeking advice on their home improvement projects.

Job Description 2: Local home improvement store seeks warm body to give pretend answers to home improvement questions. Must be adept at quick referrals to non-existent employees that you will pretend are on the opposite side of the store, allowing you time to go to the break room and wait until your customer has left the store. Applicants with real building experience need not apply.

It's basically the luck of the draw as to which employee you get and, sometimes, the only way to tell is to ask for their union card. The ones to avoid are those belonging to The International Brotherhood of Pretend Home Improvement Advisors.

As Paul progressed each day on the remodel, we learned more and more about our house. It appeared that certain parts of the house were built quite well, but there were other parts that looked as if the previous owner would have challenged me for the title of 7th grade Shop Klutz. One electrical panel would be pristine and then we'd discover another that was a jumbled mess of wires that bore a striking resemblance to a plate of angel hair spaghetti. Our

ceiling and many interior walls looked spectacular with their perfectly laid cedar planks, but our do-it-yourself previous owner had put up an outdoor spa building that was like a large-scale version of my uninhabitable cat house.

One of the fun little discoveries we made was that we had our very own well. We actually knew this when we bought the house and I remember vividly how we first learned about it:

Real Estate Agent: And over here, Mr. Elliott, is your well…

Me: …uh, did you say WELL? What do we need a well for?

Real Estate Agent: Well you see, Mr. Elliott, the water flow from the community water source is not very strong on your property and…

Me: Wait, is this something mechanical?

Real Estate Agent: Well, Mr. Elliott, I guess you could say…

Me: Oh Lordy, I can't do this! I'll never be able to keep this running! Just ask my 7th Grade shop teacher!

Once I had calmed down, I was assured that there are people who would help us make sure the well was operating properly and that I wouldn't, through mechanical incompetence, poison myself and my entire family. As it turns out, I was not underestimating the challenge ahead. Even Paul spent days studying all the valves, pipes, meters and gizmos in our well house trying to make sure that the first time he turned on the water it would not flood the entire house. He looked at all those stacked boxes in our garage and I'm sure he could envision the floating debris from what easily could become his own Hurricane Katrina.

Eventually the water got turned on, everything stayed dry and, so far, the water's still on. I'm just hoping I'll never have to look at the inside of that well house again.

17

Deer Roulette

Much of the remodeling was done in a couple of months, although there is a long line of small projects we'll be working on for the foreseeable future. We still have some trim to put up, our deck needs to be refurbished and there are lots of other odds and ends that just come with buying a house. At some point, though, you have to start living in your new house and adjusting to your new life in the country.

For people moving from Southern California to the northern climes, weather can be one of the biggest adjustments. It would have been great to take up residence in the summer and gradually work our way up to the cold winter we all knew was coming. But nothing about this move was going to be easy, so why should the weather be any different? We had only been in our new house a few days before the first big snowfall arrived.

Yes, we'd grown up in this weather but our last 14 years of driving had been on Southern California freeways where five minutes of rain is treated like the Storm of the Century. There actually are two types of California drivers when it comes to the rain:

Type 1: "Hmmm, the forecast calls for showers today – I can't possibly make it into work. How can anyone drive when there is WATER on the freeway?"

Type 2: "Why slow down for a little rain?"

Neither type does well in snow and, if you're not careful, you can turn into a California driver just by living there. Exhibit A is my wife who, I must say, lost her driving mojo for a while because she would never get to drive in the snow. We'd visit places with snow and I would do the driving, and just like a pilot who needs to keep flying to maintain his skills, I was maintaining a certain level of competence by driving in the snow. Meanwhile, my wife was getting rusty. I found it interesting that my wife – who wanted to move to the snowy Northwest more than I did – had just one rule when we arrived at our new house: "I do not want to drive in the snow."

Once that first snowfall came, it was tough just getting our vehicles out of our driveway. It soon became apparent that the price of our new house was going to be $700 higher than anticipated because of the purchase of a brand-new industrial grade snow blower. This is one rugged machine and, for all those men out there needing a little shot of masculinity, this is the perfect device for that. You start it up and it's loud and mean and just maintaining control of it is like holding onto a Brahma bull. It takes a real man to run a snow blower, unlike those little weenie electric mowers my California neighbors use.

The snow blower is cool, but someday I might even buy a tractor. A tractor with a snow blade is the ultimate act of independence and means that you will never have to rely on anyone to help you get out of your driveway. Another variation is to attach the snow blade to a four-wheeler, which means you can use the four-wheeler for hunting and fishing in the back country. All my new neighbors seem to have one or the other and, if you haven't figured it out already, my neighborhood is chockfull of good old boys and their toys.

Once out of the driveway, the two-lane road to town from our house is narrow, snowy and icy during winter storm season – which is bad enough, but then you have to think about the deer. During fall and winter the deer come down from the high country to offer themselves up to hunters and to be run over by local motorists. Deer have a knack for choosing just the right moment to step out in front of a car and commit hari-kari. It's as if they're waiting by the side of a road, timing their collision with a stop-watch: "Okay, here comes a car, Bambi, get ready – you gotta time this just right – okay, here you go -- three, two, one – go!"

We had not encountered many deer in San Diego so we weren't really thinking about them on one of our first after-dark trips to town from our new house. All of a sudden a very big deer jumps out in front of our Jeep like it came from nowhere – I can still recall that final image of the deer in full stride and then the collision a nano-second later. In the back seat my sister-in-law screamed. In the front seat, my wife had that deer-in-the-headlights look. And then this apparently very hearty deer scampered off leaving behind a couple thousand dollars in damage to our front end.

Get Ready Bambi....

From that point on, every trip to town was an adventure. Deer would play Let's Scare The Humans along the most unlikely stretches of roadway, popping out from behind trees, from behind bushes, in groups of two or three, sometimes in herds of seven or eight. Some would send a decoy deer out first to make us think that was the only one – we'd slow down for it, then speed up when it was passed and along would come ANOTHER deer. For us, every trip to town became a game of Deer Roulette, wondering if this was the trip we would hit another deer.

Over time, this took a toll on my wife. A devout Roman Catholic, she instituted a Safe Driving Prayer that she would recite at the beginning of every trip out of our driveway. It started off simple enough, something to the effect: "Dear Lord, please don't let us hit another deer because we can't afford to spend $2,000 every time we go to the store." Gradually, the prayer lengthened to include protection for everybody in the car from every possible mishap, and then it expanded to include protection for all of our relatives even though they were nowhere near the car. Eventually the prayer became longer than most trips to the store and she could be seen finishing up her prayer just as she showed her membership card to the greeter at Costco. "We ask this in your name, dear Lord – oh, just a minute, I've got my Costco card right here – in Jesus's name, amen."

Actually, with any luck, there will be fewer trips to Costco in the future. There is nothing inherently bad about Costco except that everything we buy there is in triple the quantity that we need. A family of three just does not need to buy four dozen hamburger buns and the only option is to throw out what you don't use or fill up your freezer with hamburger buns. Multiply this times hundreds of items that we buy at Costco and you see the problem. "But do you realize how little we pay per item?" my wife will always say. "It doesn't matter," I say. "If you're buying stuff you don't need you're still spending more money."

So I've asked my wife to go into Costco Rehab, a 10-step program designed to get her off bulk food purchases and live a more financially healthy life buying just the quantity of items she actually needs.

18

Small Town Living for Kids

We would give you a play-by-play description of what it's like for our 7th grade daughter to go to a small-town school except that we are not permitted within a two-mile radius of the school due to our daughter's paralyzing fear that someone at school might actually see her with her parents. The last time we went for a parent-teacher conference it felt like we were being put in the Witness Protection Program as she intercepted us at the door and whisked us through secret unused back hallways to a classroom where the desks and chairs were the only sign that kids had ever passed this way. "Don't talk to any kids!" she reminded us just on the chance we would see someone under the age of 30.

But we can tell you what country schools are like based on our own formative years, growing up in a town of 1,000 souls that included approximately 978 gossips. Most everything in a small town is about what everybody else does and being able to tell someone about it. You might think that moving to the country will make you more anonymous, but that's not so – especially for kids.

I could sit down and write you a list of the 31 people in my graduating class and tell you who's smart, who's dumb, who's clumsy, who's cool and whether they prefer beer or hard liquor. When the FBI does a background check on someone from a small town, they know that all they have to do is find a classmate who has spent 12 years going through school with the person in question and they'll find out just about everything they need to know.

That's because in a small town, first-graders are pretty much given a life sentence when they show up for school the first day: "Little Johnny, meet the people you will live, breathe and grow old with for the next 12 years." Johnny's not going to get rid of these people until he graduates and, even then, it can be hard to shake some of them. In larger cities, kids may hang with the same group of kids for a few grades but, chances are, the first big break will come in Middle School when everyone is sent off to a different building, maybe even a different school and certainly a different group of kids in the classroom.

But in a small town everyone moves through life together – which means you have to be very careful about your interpersonal relationships. If you get labeled a deviant in first grade, the first thing someone will say at your 10 year high school reunion is: "Do you remember what a deviant little Johnny was?" With the same 20 or 30 people in your class, it won't take long for you to alienate everyone in class, so one of the first lessons you learn is to never be completely honest about yourself. In the words of that famous Gillette commercial: "Never let them see you sweat."

Sometimes your deepest secrets will come out anyway. We had one particular classmate who had trouble keeping up in our various reading assignments and other homework and his academic challenges soon earned him the thoughtful, compassionate nickname of "Dumbest." I think he eventually became a hard-working, contributing member of society but the one thing he probably never put on his resume was his school nickname.

Now if Dumbest had been from a large school, it's possible he could have contained the problem and been given a clean slate when he started up with a new set of classmates. In a small town, forget about it – once you have a nickname it basically becomes a permanent part of your high school transcripts. "I see here in your transcripts that you went by the name of Dumbest. Do you care to explain to us here at Higher Education University just why we should still let you be part of this year's freshman class?"

If you're a kid in a small town, you're always looking for something to do. Truthfully, a lot of small-town kids focus on athletics or extra-curricular activities or work after school. But there is always some time during the weekend to get into some mischief and it's not like you can just hop in your car and go down to the local shopping mall. In my home town we came up with the novel idea of rafting on the local sewage lagoon. We were grade-school age and would hike a mile out of town to the reservoir where, as you might imagine, there was never anyone around. It could have been the disgusting odor, or the unique objects found floating in the lagoon that kept people away, or maybe it was just because most people knew it was illegal to be there. But, for us, this was prime lakefront property and we had it all to ourselves.

For those of us below a certain age, the pieces of latex material that kept getting caught up in our paddles served as a kind of conversation-starter for discussions we had with older kids who divulged to us various anatomical details about the opposite sex. None of us had really thought through this whole boy-girl thing and, near as we could tell, girls were different from us only in that they liked to play with dolls and we liked to poke each other's eyes out. But a couple of Saturdays out on the raft and we basically came away as trained sex therapists.

As a kid in a small town, you also gain a certain familiarity with local police officers – and they with you. In our town there were only 300 kids to keep an eye on, kindergarten through high school, and the cops got to know you through various activities such as Boy Scouts, basketball and football games, school dances, church functions and underage keg parties. Whenever there was an infraction, there was no need to check fingerprints or DNA to identify the culprit – the investigating officer most likely had been the unsub's scoutmaster, ball coach or stepfather.

This familiarity also meant that the local constables were tuned into the street – nothing happened without the cops eventually knowing about it. Just about everyone who wasn't doing anything was a snitch and, at the first sign of trouble, the first person caught would fold like a chair, quickly ratting out the other evil-doers. A case in point was the Great Beer Scandal of my senior year when a significant portion of my class – yours truly included – was caught red-handed with newly purchased cases of beer. This was not the result of a long, painstaking investigation or incredibly good detective work, but rather the fruit of one interview in which our supplier gave up all his customers so quickly the investigating officer wasn't sure if he had even asked the question yet.

Fortunately, none of us had to do hard time but that might have been preferable to the police escort I was given to my dad's place of work where I had the rather unenviable task of explaining to this kind, decent man that his only son, the product of 17 years of love and spiritual guidance and the beneficiary of a good portion of his earthly wealth, was now officially a common criminal. Okay, half my classmates were, too, which was my only consolation. It had been like a modern-day Passover with the County Sheriff's Department driving through our little town, skipping every house where there was a sign on the door that read "Our first-born has no social life" and then

dragging the rest of us down the street by our thumbs to face the wrath of our unsuspecting parents.

The penalty for my transgression was the loss of my driver's license for 60 days, which in teenager years was roughly equivalent to an adult lifetime. Never mind that I lived just four blocks from school and that my major transportation need was getting myself those four blocks to school and back again. I had lost my wheels! It was like a cowboy losing his horse! Like Neil Armstrong losing his Apollo space capsule!

I suffered through the indignity of walking for those 60 days and took solace in the fact that most of my friends were walking, too. We were, after all, growing up in a small town and this was just one more example of how we were moving through life together.

19

Guns and Religion

No doubt about it, the attitudes in a small town can be quite different from your typical big city, and nowhere are the differences quite as stark as in the way small-town people look at their guns and religion.

Growing up in a small town in Washington state, guns were just part of everyday life back in the '60s and '70s. This began early in life and, if a young boy didn't get cap guns and holsters as baby shower gifts, he most certainly would have them just as soon as he had legs long enough to walk. By the time he entered school, he most likely had a BB gun and then two or three years later he graduated to a .22 rifle. Deer hunting and bird hunting entered the picture in maybe the sixth grade, so the typical boy showing up for his first year of Middle School already had an arsenal comprised of a BB gun, a .22 rifle, a 12-guage shotgun and a 30-06 rifle. Fast forward to the 21st Century and one can imagine what these now grown-up kids have to say about efforts to limit their purchase of guns. They would be more inclined to support a bill requiring every household in the U.S. to buy and maintain an M101 105mm Howitzer cannon.

But it's not hard to understand why people from more densely populated areas might not share this affinity with guns. The country kid can get to the edge of town easily, as we did, and shoot targets at the local garbage dump whereas the city kid would seem to have fewer options. "Let's go shooting today, guys – where do you want to go, your house or my house? I put up a really cool target on our back fence and the bullets hardly ever go into our neighbor's yard."

In the country it's fairly commonplace to see someone carrying a rifle, most likely on their way to or from the hunting grounds, or maybe taking a gun in for maintenance. If you see that in the city, you automatically assume it's another Lee Harvey Oswald. "Martha, call the police! There's a man with a GUN!"

It's just different in the country. One of our new neighbors introduced himself to us by telling the story of how he heard some people walking down a trail on the back of his property and he grabbed his .307 rifle to go say hello. This neighbor routinely wears camouflage attire so one gets the feeling that when he comes out to greet you with his .307, he's not exactly saying "Welcome to the neighborhood!" As it turns out, the two hikers came out with their hands up, one of them holding up photo identification indicating they were federal agents looking for a pot-growing operation in the hills out back of my neighbor's house. My neighbor stood down.

Here in the country we do, in fact, have something in common with the inner-city: it's not uncommon to hear gunfire in our neighborhood. When we moved to this house we did ask the neighbor in camo attire if it was okay to fire off our guns on our property. His response: "It's your property, ain't it?" After a while you start to get used to the gunfire that can happen just about any time of day around here, and you eventually lose that first inclination to think that your neighbor has just murdered his wife.

Religion is another big part of the country culture. Not that it's any less important to many city folks, but in a small town it's one of the key identifiers. In other words, a person is often defined by the groups he belongs to, and the order of importance in a small town is generally something like this: family, church, 4-H Club, local athletic team and Friday Night Poker Club. Your family might have the worst reputation in the county, and you might even be a swindler or crook, but if you belong to one or more of the other groups, your reputation will remain intact.

Generally speaking, there are no grand cathedrals located in small towns, and congregations can be pretty small. Most everyone going to a small town church is pressed into service like at the Episcopal Church where I can vividly recall my mother playing the organ and my father taking the collection while I did my duty as an acolyte whose chief responsibility was to not spill the wine as I helped our minister prepare for Holy Communion. On a good day, our church attendance included about eight other people, seven of whom could potentially be receiving their Last Rites.

I do have to give my parents credit. They not only were faithful servants of the Lord -- offering up not only their own services but those of their indentured servant son – but they also saw to it that we at least got a little something back. This particular church had a small recreation hall that was almost never used –our aging congregants could barely muster enough strength just to come to Sunday services – and that presented an opportunity. In about the seventh grade my parents bought me an electric guitar and amplifier and, after listening to my dissonant chords being played at an excruciating volume, they suggested that I take my amplifier and guitar to the church recreation hall and play to my heart's content. That sounded good to me, and soon I was joined by a drummer, a keyboardist, and a rather intriguing bunch of 13-year-old female groupies who, of course, were only there to get closer to the Lord.

The small-town Catholic church we attend today has a few more people than we had growing up, but the Saturday night service we go to does not have much participation from the congregants. There is no choir or organist and the service is in both English and Spanish so what we have here is a Priest-Musical Director who must not only lead every song without musical accompaniment, but do it partially in English and partially in Spanish, and then conduct the entire service alternating between the two languages. If this guy ever leaves, our church will be in trouble: "Wanted: Priest who can sing in two languages, read in two languages, talk in two languages, direct acolytes not to spill the wine and work for peanuts."

20

Yard Work

Perhaps one of the most jarring aspects about moving to the country is the quantum leap you take from mowing a postage-stamp sized lawn once a week to continually maintaining your new "acreage." When you first look at the pictures of your new six-acre property, all you can think about is how cool it would be to live in the middle of your own park, a kind of nature preserve that, like all of God's eco-systems, pretty much takes care of itself.

Wrong.

What you should be thinking about is what it will be like working as the park custodian for no pay, digging holes, planting vegetation, trimming plants and trees – and, yes, mowing a vastly larger lawn – while all of your friends in your former neighborhood are playing golf, traveling or simply relaxing with their feet up in the Man Cave watching sports and drinking beer. In all of our pre-move discussions about getting a big piece of property it's funny, but I don't remember my wife even once bringing up the fact that taking on acreage was only slightly less of a commitment than having another child.

Now it took a while for all of this to sink in. As you'll recall, we moved in pretty close to the dead of winter with snow falling shortly after our arrival. All those plants, trees and grass were quickly covered with snow and looked more like a Christmas postcard than the endless beautification project that they would eventually become. Yes, I was quickly saddled with the responsibility of blowing snow from our way-too-long driveway but somehow, in my mind, that was going to be my major commitment to this new property and thus I was in no danger of losing time in the Man Cave.

When spring arrived, the snow receded to reveal a layer of pine needles and pine cones, fallen branches and whole lot of trees that needed trimming. There were shrubs and brush everywhere, tangled vines and lots of sick plants that were basically on life support due to the previous owner's lack of attention. We had some of these issues on our previous property which, by Southern California standards, was a humungous 1/3 acre. But by my calculations, we now had approximately 18 times as much acreage including an annoying forest of trees that insists on continually shedding or dropping this or that, requiring constant surveillance in order to keep our property from looking like the Wenatchee National Forest's equivalent of Detroit.

Now don't get me wrong – I still try to get out of as much of this work as I can. Since I work from my home, it's amazing how there is always something extremely urgent for me to finish at my computer just at the time my wife is hinting very strongly that it would be nice if I came out and helped her carry some yard waste or complete some other inane, thoroughly unfulfilling yard task.

Wife: Can you come out and help me carry that brush over to the fire pit?

Me: Be right there, dear, after I call Hong Kong because they can only be reached at this hour and, oh that's right, I also have to write up that proposal before Mr. Big leaves the office for the day – oh and I almost forgot I have to change the ink cartridge on the copier and I'm not quite sure how to do it so I will have to go search for the manual and then read it all the way through to make sure I'm completely sure I'm doing it right. But shouldn't take too long, dear…

The other thing you have to realize about buying acreage is that every square inch will have to be decorated – at least that's the rule according to Mrs. Elliott's Handbook for Moving to a New House. Now most men would be satisfied with a neon beer sign flashing through the front window as prominently as possible, but many females take nesting far more seriously than that. In our house, decorations are not a joint decision because I'm a man and obviously I have no taste. It's a much more secretive, insidious process whereby my wife will start putting out a few decorations here and there in a way that I, being a man, probably will not even notice – at first.

It starts with a couple of fake flowers planted inconspicuously alongside the back of the house or along some pathway that is hardly ever used. Then you start to notice a few gnomes popping up here and there, and then come a few small statues of naked cherubs, the occasional angel, a porcelain mushroom or two, flower pots and two-foot-high porcelain frogs. So apparently my wife was going for some kind of Fairy Tale-Biblical-National Geographic motif which she and other women must have learned in their 7th Grade Home Economics and Decorating class while I was barely eking out a grade in 7th Grade Shop. For my money, I'd rather just have the beer sign but I can always put that up just before my bro friends come to visit.

Me: Hey guys, thanks for coming out. Can't wait to throw down a few tall ones, kick back and watch the game…

Bro Friends: Hey, man, good to see you, too. Love the beer sign. But dude… you gotta lose the gnomes and cherubs. What is this, the Enchanted Forest??

21

Small Town Workers

Moving to rural America, you do discover that you are leaving behind a certain amount of efficiency that just comes with having so many people in the Big City scrambling to compete with each other for enough work to pay the higher cost of living in the city. It's do or die for the typical rat race employee, but when you get to the boonies, let's just say there are fewer options in the labor pool.

We hinted at this earlier when we told you the story of our local movers who were quite diligent about staying in touch with us throughout the Hostage Crisis but then, when it came time to actually show up for work, they were Missing In Action. That was somewhat inconvenient for us since we had the Mother of All Moving Trucks packed to the gills with household belongings that had been stored away from air and sunlight so long that there was the very real risk they would crumble into dust whenever we once again opened the back of the truck.

We had other experiences that led us to believe the issue might actually be systemic rather than one flakey mover not showing up for a day's work.

Probably our first experience with this was when we arranged to have our internet satellite disk installed. As you might guess, there is no high-speed internet out here and just one company offers any sort of alternative – a satellite dish that they set up on your property. Coming from the Big City, I planned well ahead of time and scheduled the installation to occur before we actually moved into the house. The internet company said they'd be out on X day, sometime in the morning, and I drove the 23 miles from my in-laws' house to sit in the new house and wait for them. Now this was not sitting on a couch watching TV until they came; this was sitting on the stairs because there WAS no couch or TV and basically staring at the living room wall. Late in the morning they called to say the mission was an abort – the guy couldn't come up that day because he ran into issues on another installation. The installation was rescheduled for a week later.

At the appointed time I again made the 23-mile trip to sit in our new house and stare at the wall while I waited for the installer to show up "sometime in the afternoon." About 7 p.m., a different installer shows up, flashlight in hand, to investigate locations outside the house where he can install the satellite dish. Big surprise, he comes back in the house and says it's too dark to install it tonight and asks if we can reschedule, which is kind of like the surgeon saying "I'm fresh out of anesthetics, do you mind if we re-schedule the surgery?" What are we going to say?

On the third trip, yet another installer shows up and, at this point, we believe we have met this company's entire installation department and could probably fit right in at their company picnic. The third installer then proceeds to dig a hole next to our house, pour cement and erect a dish on a pole in the only location that he says could possibly pick up the internet signal. Once installed, he proceeds to test his hypothesis and, of course, cannot get a signal. He calls his superiors, they speak in hushed tones, and then he just sort of leaves, saying something about the company will be in touch.

Weeks go by and we hear nothing from this company, which is particularly problematic because this is the only internet company that serves our area and my home business is based on the internet. Just when we're thinking we may have to set up a local office in town in order to have internet coverage, we hear from the company that a fourth installer will be coming out.

The fourth installer does show up on time and immediately pronounces the third installer incompetent – apparently he was a trainee out on his first solo install – and completely changes the dish location to another part of the property. The fourth time is the charm. After weeks of missed appointments, late arrivals and bungled installs, we finally had our internet service up and running – although, I must tell you, it's only slightly better than dial-up, and when we try to run two devices at the same time, the whole system goes into meltdown. (Forget my business, the internet service I really need is the Teen-age Girl Plan that would allow my daughter to simultaneously carry on conversations in Facebook, text her friends, video conference with hot boyfriends and play god-awful music which, she says, all help her get her homework done.)

We had one other experience with the local labor force when our contractor friend Paul hired someone to help him lay down some tile. The first couple of days went pretty well and we were getting to know this young fellow and his dog, who he says he always takes on jobs with him. Things were going so well Paul paid him at the end of the second day and he told us he would be back the next morning. Come the third day the worker was nowhere to be found, not even a call to let us know he wasn't coming. Either he met with some sort of foul play or, more likely, it was just business as usual for someone who apparently has more needy customers than competitors.

22

Into the Wild

As we were adjusting to our new address out in the country, I kept friends and family updated on Facebook about our big move "into the Wild." While I was joking about the comparison with the book and movie about the young twenty-something who walked into the Alaskan wilderness to live and who later died of starvation, the first hunger pangs for a Meat-lover's pizza from Pizza Hut made me realize there were, in fact, similarities between our situation and that naïve young man. We had both chosen to tempt fate by putting distance between us and civilization and, while we weren't yet shooting local game for survival, we were making the oil companies rich with our trips into town to satisfy our increasing appetite for any kind of food that wasn't being served up by the local forest rangers.

We had gone ahead and signed up for a DISH satellite television receiver so the illusion was that we were still close enough to town to actually go to the restaurants that were showing high-definition close-ups of every kind of food we now craved. We began longing for the days when we would see an Applebee's TV commercial and be able to act on the impulse to scarf down two entrees and a dessert for twenty bucks. Now every decision about where and what to eat had to be coldly calculated in terms of how much distance we would have to travel to enjoy a particular meal. When you're figuring on spending $40 to eat out, adding $20 in gas expenses seemed like the same kind of brilliant economic thinking we might expect from Congress.

Even without the extra gas expense, we were finding that some things just cost more in these small country towns. For example, we ordered our first Subway sandwiches here in Central Washington expecting that, since the cost of living here is cheaper, then obviously the Subway sandwiches would be, too. But we had forgotten to take into account the Rural Washington It-Costs-More-To-Get-It-Here tax that automatically adds $2 to the cost of any Subway sandwich. Some fast food joints go even further, attempting to recover the suffocating amount of money they pay for such things as water. We had spent $40 for lunch at a local hamburger stand but when one of our kids asked for a cup of water, he was told that would be 50 cents, thank you.

For our teenage daughter perhaps the biggest adjustment to living out in the country was being out of cell phone coverage. As it happens, the cell coverage ends about three miles before our house and then picks up about a mile from our house in the other direction. For our daughter, this was like taking up residence in a cosmic Black Hole where, instead of talking with friends, playing Angry Birds and downloading inane music onto her phone, she would be forced to do such humiliating things as carry on a conversation with her parents and, every so often, read a book. It is possible to get cell coverage by climbing the mountains behind our house straight up for approximately one mile and, whenever she would complain, we would remind her of this opportunity to talk with her friends and stay in shape at the same time.

Living out in the country, everything now had to be pre-planned. We were making weekly runs into Wenatchee for groceries and other supplies, but the 90-minute roundtrip was not something we wanted to do too often. We developed shopping lists, not only for groceries but for any other sort of supplies that might run out before the next trip into town. Despite her graduation from Costco Rehab, my wife was still buying some items in large quantities just to make sure we wouldn't run out. Toilet paper comes immediately to mind.

Pizza quickly became a big issue because we haven't yet found a pizza delivery guy willing to spend an hour and a half driving to and from our house, even if we do tip well. And let's face it, pizza doesn't keep. Sometime about 30 minutes after you take a pizza from the oven it turns into a big round piece of cardboard with cold cheese on it, and once past that point, there's just no defibrillating that pizza back to life. Our solution was to start buying take-and-bake pizzas which my wife would buy on her shopping trips while I stayed home to work for the day. The only problem was that my wife would get sidetracked shopping for cherubs and porcelain mushrooms, and even take-and-bake pizza gets old if you leave it out in the car all day. On certain hot days, the pizza would arrive home not only fully baked, but already in full rigor mortis.

Since out here in the forest we don't happen to have a local branch of Wells Fargo Bank, we also have to plan our banking and other errands carefully. Fortunately, we are only 20 minutes from a smaller town that does have a bank and a few stores and restaurants so not every modern convenience is completely out of reach. Quite honestly, the best local resource is Walmart, located in Chelan, the small town closest to us. For my wife, shifting allegiance from Costco to Walmart has taken her through all the stages of grief as she finally has come to accept that she may never again be able to order Costco pizza by the slice. It doesn't help that some of our Southern California friends view Walmart as a kind of interactive zoo where they can view rednecks, hay seeds, country bumpkins and other species in their native habitat. But truth be told, we even shopped at Walmart while living in Southern California – wearing fake mustaches, of course, so our friends wouldn't recognize us.

Actually, this Walmart is quite the anomaly. We are accustomed to the Southern California Walmart stores where even on a slow day it is mass pandemonium and a 10-minute walk to the store from the nearest parking spot. This Walmart is just as big and seems to have just as much merchandise but there never seems to be more than a couple dozen cars in the parking lot. You could throw a bowling ball down most aisles without hitting anyone. The store also has branched out into providing such services as eye care and hairstyling and I must say the last $15 hairstyling I got at Walmart was every bit as good as the $100 scalpings I used to endure in La Jolla.

If you're looking for entertainment out in the country, you might be surprised at what passes for fun. The first summer in our new country house I hosted a bunch of guy friends of mine (some of whom were naval veterans of those days rafting the sewage lagoon) and, while previous annual get-togethers have been held on yachts in the San Juans or on San Diego Bay, this event took place largely on my front porch. Sitting in our porch chairs looking for all the world like we could be just waiting for our still to finish a cycle of moonshine, we stared for what seemed like hours at the cat in our front yard trying to jump three times his length to grab butterflies off a lilac bush. Yes, gone were those boyhood days of fast cars and even faster women.

We do get some interesting community festivals in this part of the country and they're well worth coming down from the mountain to see. The Washington State Apple Blossom Festival in Wenatchee is one example, an 11-day celebration of spring that includes a two-hour-long Grand Parade. Growing up in this part of the country, this was our Rose Parade with miles of streets set aside for an impressive display of parade entries. There are a lot of fun things to watch in the parade, including great marching bands, floats and equestrian groups but it's also the kind of parade that if you start a new landscaping business in town, they'll just have you drive your lawn mower down the parade route and wave to the sometimes puzzled parade-goers.

One of the highlights of this parade is the horse dancing where riders somehow train their horses to do a kind of tap-dance routine while they're trotting down the parade route. I'm watching this and then suddenly I flashed on what it would be like if there was a Planet of the Horses where the horses rode us humans and made us tap-dance our way down a three-mile parade route full of wildly enthusiastic horses clapping their hooves while we humans were put through these ridiculous paces.

And then I committed not one, but two faux pas– both reminders we were now living in a small town.

The first had to do with the Apple Blossom Festival itself. There are 10 princess finalists for Apple Blossom and three of those are selected as the Queen and her Court. There are four other princesses out of the 10 that follow the Queen and her Court down the parade route in separate cars, each with some sort of special award designation. Then the final car has the three leftover princesses. "They might as well put up a big sign that says Our Three Non-Prize Winners," I announced, "or maybe they could be kind and just label them Undrafted Princesses."

"Shhhh!" my wife whispered in horror. "One of the girls' families is sitting right next to us!"

A little while later the P.A. announcer made a joking reference to the Mr. Ed television show and I, of course, couldn't keep my mouth shut. "That's the problem with hiring an old guy to do the announcing," I said. "Not many people here even know who Mr. Ed is!"

"Shhhh!" my wife whispered again. "The lady sitting right in front of us is the announcer's mother!"

There's not much night life in these parts, but we do have an Indian casino about a half-hour away and one weekend we got a wild hair to go down and listen to some live music. The problem with casinos is that they have slot machines, which have a tendency to drown out the music. Plus, the local tribe is exempt from laws prohibiting smoking. So our fun night out at the casino consisted of a 60-minute round-trip drive on narrow country roads, music we could not quite hear, a band we could not quite see through the smoky haze and, due to a temporary medical issue, beer I could not quite drink.

23

Outdoor Recreation

One of the reasons we moved to the country is that we've always loved various forms of outdoor recreation and, let's face it, you can't get much more outdoors than living in the wilderness. I can look outside my home office window and see steep rocky cliffs that may not be as high as El Capitan, but certainly look as daunting. Not that I would ever dare in my wildest dreams or weakest moments of irrationality even consider climbing up a mountain any higher that I can reach on a step-ladder.

My wife, on the other hand, thinks she is a rock climber. She's never bought any gear or learned how to pound in those staple thingies that allow one to actually have something to hold onto. No, she prefers to climb daredevil style, without a net. She finds little places where the rock looks solid enough to step onto, and then basically hopes that it will not give way as she shifts all her weight and gambles her entire future existence on the idea that this rock will not choose this particular moment to send her tumbling to the ground below. I used to have a tendency to yell at her from the ground to "be careful" but every time I did that, she would slip a little bit. So now I just close my eyes and mentally rehearse how I am going to run quickly to the drop zone and spread my body out on the ground to create a kind of human mattress for her to fall on.

She will claim she takes no chances but I do have one episode that would seem to support my constant admonitions that she should, at this mature stage of her life, take up something less dangerous -- say, needlepoint. We were visiting Yosemite when our youngest daughter was about three years old and we walked a short distance to the viewing area of one of the spectacular falls. My wife decided she wanted to join the more adventurous park visitors and climb a narrow mountainside trail up to the falls. I, of course, declined – but she insisted on taking our daughter. Soon there was a bit of commotion in the viewing area where I was waiting:

Someone in the crowd: Do you see that woman up there with that little child – what does she think she's doing?

Someone else in the crowd: Oh, I can't believe this. That's child abuse! There's always going to be some idiot out there.

Me: Yes, you're right! She should be arrested and they should throw away the key! By the way, I don't know that woman and have never seen her before in my life!

Of course she will just point to my own forms of recreation that don't always turn out as one would expect. Probably chief among those is boating, the kind of sport I love because it basically involves sitting in a chair and turning a steering wheel while you soak up the sun and get sprayed with water just often enough to keep you cooled down. The only problem with boating is that part of it is mechanical and, for me, that means an automatic surcharge because I don't dare try and maintain the boat myself.

We've had boats forever and perhaps the very first time I ever went boating was an omen. I remember it as if it was yesterday and I believe I was the first documented case of PTBSD (Post Traumatic Boat Stress Disorder), diagnosed later in life when it continued to affect my relationship with boats. I was 11 years old and my dad had bought a $1 raffle ticket at the local fair and low and behold he won the prize – a 14-foot Fiberform boat with a 35 horsepower Gale motor. My mom, dad and I couldn't wait to put it in the water and, dripping with anticipation, we took it to a local lake and backed it down the launch ramp for the very first time. Everything was going well as we lowered the boat down into the water and my dad drove the car and trailer to the parking lot. But just then we noticed that our new boat was sitting a little low in the water. Wait a minute, I thought, something's not right. Is there supposed to be six inches of water on the floor of the boat? Nearby onlookers, who by now were yelling for my dad to bring the trailer back, assured me this was not normal. They quickly surmised that we had failed to follow Rule No. 1 of boating: Always Put The Drain Plug Back In Your Boat. We were taking on water faster than the Titanic.

These kinds of experiences seemed to continue over the years. Fast Forward about 30 years and I had graduated to a 38-foot Bayliner yacht, a boat we leased through a yacht share program that split the cost between six families.

I decided it was time to impress my buddies with a yacht trip through the San Juan Islands and we set out from Anacortes, Washington, with the same innocent, naïve expectation that everything would go all right as I'm sure Gilligan and the Captain had leaving for their two-hour tour. A day or so later we're cruising through some inlets on San Juan Island with my buddy at the helm while I'm below deck being the life of the party, secretly pretending that my bloodline flowed directly through the Hamptons and that this yachting stuff was just an everyday thing for me. Then my buddy yells down to the cabin: "Here, Chas, you take the helm." I step up to the bridge and take the wheel and, 15 seconds later, we hear a deep scraping sound on the hull.

Now scraping is not something you want to hear in a boat. It can mean many things, almost all of them bad. In this case, it meant that we had charted a course directly onto a submerged rock that had just cut a rather unsightly gash in the gel coat on our hull. Long story short, that meant a haul-out for repairs and that meant my three-day weekend with the Boys was going to cost me something on the order of $62.50 an hour for every hour we were away from the dock, including the time we slept.

And then there's the time we bought a 28-foot Bayliner. Being diligent consumers, we had the boat thoroughly inspected and pronounced completely seaworthy. In hindsight, we think that this particular boat inspector had been a real estate inspector in a past life because it didn't take but two outings before this boat's outdrive broke down and our $30,000 boat was now costing us a total of $40,000 and change because we now had to tack on the cost of rebuilding the outdrive.

You would think that we've had enough boating by now, but our new house in the country is just minutes from 55-mile-long Lake Chelan and not having a boat here would be like living at the airport and having no airplane. So we bought an 18-foot Sea Ray, had it inspected by someone with no discernible real estate background, and we now make it a point each day to go out and check to make sure the plug is still in the boat.

24

The Top 10 Lessons

Sometimes you have to wait decades for history to tell whether a president was really successful, and so it is with telling the story of your home purchase, remodel and cross-country move. For one thing, the remodel never stops – well at least it hasn't in our case – and, for another, it takes time to see how well you're going to adjust to your new environment. And, from a purely financial standpoint, your success or failure pretty much depends on whether you were able to get someone else to buy your house for a price that made your home investment worthwhile. Check back with us in a few years and we'll let you know.

For us, the move was motivated primarily by wanting to get closer to aging parents and growing grandkids and, judged by just those two measurements, the move could be considered a success. My wife is getting much more quality time with her parents and, even though they still live a three-hour drive away, the grandkids are finding plenty of uses for our larger property and the nearby lake. The kids are showing up just often enough to remember who we are, but not so often we have to get a daycare license.

But there have been lessons learned, and here are the Top 10 Biggest Lessons we've learned – so far -- from our move to the country:

Lesson No. 10 – Don't ever move.

It dawned on us somewhere between the Hostage Crisis and the systematic transferral of nearly all our liquid assets to Home Depot that we had been awfully happy in our house in Southern California. If you don't move, you will never even have to TALK to a real estate agent and, when you're gone, your heirs will enjoy combing through all those boxes in your garage finding hidden treasures that pre-date civilization.

Lesson No. 9 – We're in the wrong occupation.

Forget about becoming a doctor or a lawyer or a Wall Street titan – you'll be much farther ahead if you study hard to become a home inspector. Don't cut the classes where they teach you how to hook up with a successful realtor to ensure lots of repeat business.

Lesson No. 8 – Might as well rob a bank.

A "pre-approval" for real estate financing, these days, is like getting a pre-diploma from the college you want to attend. It doesn't mean much until you've actually done the coursework, and your loan pre-approval doesn't mean much until your lender has actually put you through a series of tests not dissimilar to the prisoner interrogations at Gitmo.

Lesson No. 7 – We're not championship boxers.

Don't let anyone tell you boxing is easy, especially when you're boxing up a lifetime of memories that, presumably, you want to see again someday. Even my sister-in-law, who could compete in Olympic boxing, made mistakes. Key revelation: label top, bottom and every side unless you want to continue lifting boxes as part of your ongoing weight training.

Lesson No. 6 – "Cheap fixer-upper" is an oxymoron.

When you're mechanically challenged, there is no such thing as a cheap fixer-upper – only a self-funded jobs program that will single-handedly put people back to work and save the local economy.

Lesson No. 5 – All cars should come with deer whistles.

If deer are going to commit Suicide By Car you'd think they would at least have the common decency not to do any damage to the car.

Lesson No. 4 – Frogs are obnoxious little creatures.

Our previous owner graciously left us his backyard water feature complete with a pond that serves as a rallying point for a colony of frogs who choose to croak loudly and incessantly only when we are trying desperately to get to sleep.

Lesson No. 3 – Status symbols in the country are different.

Whereas the primary gauge of success in our California neighborhood was whether your BMW series began with a 3 or a 7, our new neighborhood status symbol is a tractor with a snow plow.

Lesson No. 2 – There is no need to change clothes – ever.

There is a reason Larry the Cable Guy always wears the same clothes – out here you don't really have to change if you only see other human beings sporadically. This is also why the Unabomber had a rather one-dimensional wardrobe.

Lesson No. 1 – God didn't intend for us to live in the country.

Otherwise He would have extended city water and sewer lines out here and positioned an In-N-Out Burger someplace where we could actually get to it.

www.ingramcontent.com/pod-product-compliance
Lightning Source LLC
Chambersburg PA
CBHW062010040426
42447CB00010B/1990